W9-ATP-845

ΛD Architectural Design

Club Culture

Guest-edited by Eleanor Curtis

RAY KLUGA
511 AVE OF THE AMERICAS #53
NEW YORK, NY 10011

WILEY-ACADEMY

Architectural Design
Vol 73 No 6 November/December 2003

ISBN 0-47086215-7

Profile No 166

Editorial Offices
International House
Ealing Broadway Centre
London W5 5DB
T: +44 (0)20 8326 3800
F: +44 (0)20 8326 3801
E: architecturaldesign@wiley.co.uk

Editor
Helen Castle
Production
Mariangela Palazzi-Williams
Art Director
Christian K sters ⤳ CHK Design
Designer
Scott Bradley ⤳ CHK Design
Project Coordinator
Caroline Ellerby
Picture Editor
Famida Rasheed

Advertisement Sales
01243 843272

Editorial Board
Denise Bratton, Adriaan Beukers,
Andr Chaszar, Peter Cook,
Max Fordham, Massimiliano
Fuksas, Edwin Heathcote,
Anthony Hunt, Charles Jencks,
Jan Kaplicky, Robert Maxwell,
Jayne Merkel, Monica Pidgeon,
Antoine Predock, Leon van Schaik

Contributing Editors
Andr Chaszar
Craig Kellogg
Jeremy Melvin
Jayne Merkel

Abbreviated positions
b=bottom, c=centre, l=left, r=right

Front and back cover: photography © British
Airways plc

AD

pp 4-5 Lightroom / K O'Sullivan; p 6 © Karim
Rashid Inc., photo: Ramin Talaie; pp 7 & 9 ©
Richard Bryant / arcaid.co.uk; pp 10-1 ©
Dennis Gilbert / VIEW; pp 12 & 13(l) photos:
Chris Smailes; p 13(r) by Ben Jeffrey; pp 14-7
photos: © Eric Laignel; pp 18-9 & 22-3 photos:
Shigeyuki Morishita; pp 20 & 21(tl) © Unimat
Liberty, photos: Souichi Murazumi; p 21(tr)
photo: Yasushi Miyahashi; p 21(inset) photo:
Hijyun Kasuya; pp 24 & 25 photos: Benny Chan
of Fotoworks; pp 26-7 photos: Mistumasa
Fujitsuka; pp 28-31 & 33 photos: © Raymond
Dragon; pp 34-5 photos: © Wade Zimmerman
Photographer; pp 36-7 photos: © John Horner;
p 40(t) © Alex Popov, photo: Kraig Carlstrom;
p 40(b) courtesy Mitchell Library, State Library
of New South Wales, Australia; p 41 courtesy
Ancher Mortlock and Woolley, Architects; pp 42
& 44 photos: © Peter Hyatt; p 43 photo: ©
Tyrone Branigan; p 45 © Gollings Photography
P/L; pp 46-7 photos: © Patrick Bingham-Hall;
pp 49-53 photography © British Airways plc;
pp 54 & 57 © ResidenSea; p 58 © Freedom
Ship International, Inc.; pp 60-5 © Cunard;
pp 66-7 By courtesy of the Trustees of Sir John
Soane's Museum; p 68 © Martin Charles; p 69
© Wickham van Eyck Architects; pp 70-1 ©
Chassay + Last Architects; pp 72-3 © Nicola
Argent @ Gebler Tooth; pp 74-5 photos: ©
Chris Gascoigne / VIEW; p 77 © Universal
Design Studio; pp 78-9 © Valerie Bennett;
p 80(t) © David Blackburn; p 80(b) © Nigel
Coates and Why Not Associates; pp 81-3 ©
Martyn Rose-Rebecca Valentine Agency; p 84-5
Fabric photography by Tom Stapley; pp 86-7
photos: Luca Zampedri; pp 88-9 courtesy

Ashley Carter Whitehead, photos: Uli Weber;
p 91(tl) photo: Brigitte Bouillot; pp 90-3 © Ed
Reeve; pp 94 & 95(c&b) © Adjaye / Associates;
p 95(t) © Miller Hare; p 96 courtesy Louis
Vuitton, © Jimmy Cohressen.

AD+

pp 98+ & 99(l)+ © Scott B Smith; pp 100+ &
101+ © Wolf-Gordon, photos: James Shanks;
pp 102-7+ © Enrique Norton, photos: Jaime
Navarro; pp 108-16+ © Freecell; p 117-23+ ©
Gehry Partners, LLP; pp 124-5+ photos: ©
David Marks; pp 126-7+ photos: © Matteo
Piazza.

Published in Great Britain in 2003 by Wiley-
Academy, a division of John Wiley & Sons Ltd
Copyright ' 2003, John Wiley & Sons Ltd, The
Atrium, Southern Gate, Chichester, West Sussex
PO19 8SQ, England, Telephone (+44) 1243 779777
Email (for orders and customer service enquiries):
cs-books@wiley.co.uk Visit our Home Page on
www.wileyeurope.com or www.wiley.com

All Rights Reserved. No part of this publication
may be reproduced, stored in a retrieval system
or transmitted in any form or by any means, elec-
tronic, mechanical, photocopying, recording, scanning or otherwise, except under the terms
of the Copyright, Designs and Patents Act 1988
or under the terms of a licence issued by the
Copyright Licensing Agency Ltd, 90 Tottenham
Court Road, London W1T 4LP, UK, without the per-
mission in writing of the Publisher.

Requests to the Publisher should be addressed
to the Permissions Department, John Wiley &
Sons Ltd, The Atrium, Southern Gate, Chichester,
West Sussex PO19 8SQ, England, or emailed to
permreq@wiley.co.uk, or faxed to (+44) 1243 770571.

Subscription Offices UK
John Wiley & Sons Ltd.
Journals Administration Department
1 Oldlands Way, Bognor Regis
West Sussex, PO22 9SA
T: +44 (0)1243 843272
F: +44 (0)1243 843232
E: cs-journals@wiley.co.uk

Annual Subscription Rates 2003
Institutional Rate: UK £160
Personal Rate: UK £99
Student Rate: UK £70
Institutional Rate: US $240
Personal Rate: US $150
Student Rate: US $105
AD is published bi-monthly.
Prices are for six issues and include
postage and handling charges.
Periodicals postage paid at Jamaica,
NY 11431. Air freight and mailing
in the USA by Publications
Expediting Services Inc, 200 Meacham
Avenue, Elmont, NY 11003

Single Issues UK: £22.50
Single Issues outside UK: US $45.00
Details of postage and packing charges
available on request

Postmaster
Send address changes to AD Publications
Expediting Services, 200 Meacham Avenue,
Elmont, NY 11003

Printed in Italy. All prices are subject to
change without notice. [ISSN: 0003-8504]

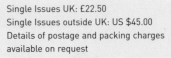

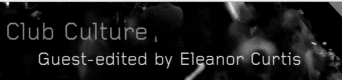

Club Culture

Guest-edited by Eleanor Curtis

∆D

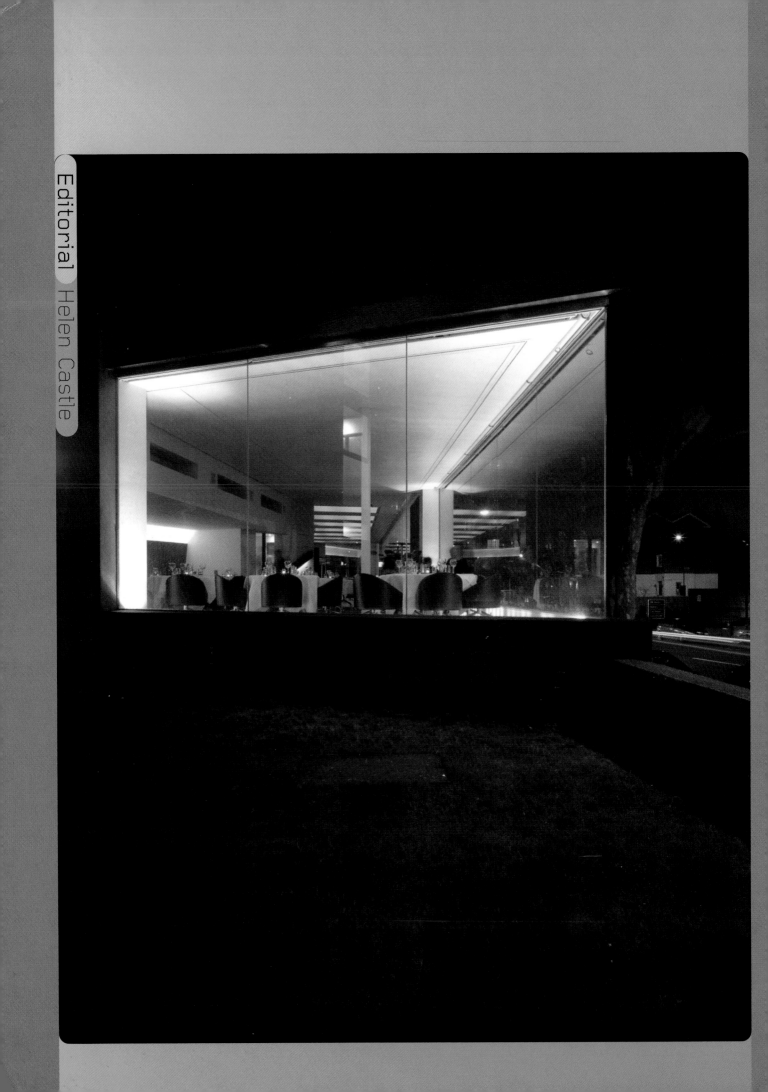

Clubs by their very nature intrigue. As the secret gardens of building types, they leave us firmly on the other side of the door with our eyes close up to the keyhole, conjecturing on what luxuries and subversive pleasures lie within. It is not, however, clubs' predilection for exclusivity that makes them such a ripe topic for △. It is the manner in which they aspire to appeal to an idealised membership and in so doing draw a line around a particular social or economic class.

This dynamic behind clubs has become sharpened and accentuated in recent years with the expansion of the leisure industry and a whole new spectrum of health and fitness clubs, and membership clubs attached to restaurants and bars. The necessity to attract a membership distinguished by wealth, rather than an interest group or even social strata has made design and the dressing up of clubs a heightened activity. Design has thus become a process of sophisticated, finely honed pitching. This is true of new and old clubs, whether they are launching themselves afresh in a grandiose manner, as Sketch did in London in the spring of 2003 with a whole showcase of star designers, or whether they are a simple makeover of an existing facility to attract a wider age range across the sexes. None, except for the most classic membership clubs, can fall back on that comfortable established design vocabulary of the traditional gentleman's club unless, of course, it is in a self-conscious or nostalgic fashion.

What actually constitutes a club has become increasingly difficult to pin down. In the last couple of decades, a thin line has developed between clubs and commerce, with clubs being increasingly run solely for commercial gain rather than in the interest of the club members. Conversely, the benefits of transferring the ambience and accoutrements of club culture into retail and the restaurant industry have also not been lost on commerce. This may simply be a matter of an individual restaurant re-creating the intimate atmosphere of a private members' club for its clientele, or of a large supermarket chain issuing 'club cards' to pull in customer loyalty. The definition of a club has thus become ever more elastic with this increasing blurring of boundaries between clubs and commerce. What, however, remains ever more present and pressing, in a transient, money-orientated world, is that sense of belonging that being a member of a club engenders – even if it is money that effectively buys you that golden ticket to announce that you are 'one of us'. △

Opposite and below
The Otto Dining Lounge Restaurant in Maida Vale, northwest London, exemplifies the infinite capacity of the contemporary city to rebrand and reinvent itself. The refurbishment and extension of a communal facility attached to a 1960s council housing block has been reincarnated by Stiff + Trevillion Architects as the 21st-century equivalent of a 19th-century Pall Mall club. Redefined by its use of luxurious modern materials – iroko, black leather and travertine – and an elegant glass extension, Otto is a wholly recreational space for dining, drinking and meeting.

Above
Designed by designer of the moment Karim Rashid, Powder Deep Studios was opened at the end of 2002 in what is currently Manhattan's hippest area, the Meatpacking District. Combining a photography studio, special events studio and nightclub in a single multilevel space, Powder offers unique amenities for private parties, fashion and music shoots. Though pitched largely as a nightclub, with music as 'the star attraction', it also has 30 tables open for reservation and places an emphasis on a high level of service from the waiting staff.

Clubs, by tradition, were private places. They excluded and selected, and as a member you felt you were part of a select few. They were typically based on particular activities (sports) or commonalities (class, nationality, gender), interests (motoring, arts) or ideologies (political), within which strict boundaries were set. As a member, you respected and reinforced these boundaries.

Architecture sometimes, though not always, played its part in defining these boundaries and gave physical identity to the club – an identity that had a reciprocal relationship with the people who aspired to becoming, and became, its members.

Today, however, in contrast to their original exclusivity, clubs are all around and membership is open to almost anyone. The club of today has adopted a much more loose definition of what it means to 'belong', deliberately blurring the boundaries of membership and thus affording more freedom for its members and, in turn, its space (if indeed it has one).

Physical form and architecture for this new breed of clubs play a different role. No longer are these only a reflection of the club's identity, but in some instances they actually define the club identity (in terms of graphic design), and in other instances have to adapt to the changing nature of its members.

Take, for example, the very successful Nectar club where membership is defined by purchasing products from Sainsbury's supermarket or filling the tank at a BP petrol station. Nectar has no

physical space with which to identify, nor a historic building to attend to affirm your membership. And yet it is perhaps one of the UK's largest clubs (it has 12 million members) and may be one of the better known. Nectar is identified by its orange credit-card-sized membership card – a simple piece of product and graphic design that holds the key to the members' data.

Clubs do not need a physical structure to give them that sense of exclusivity that makes them a club. Dress codes, music, logos and identi-cards can all help to define club membership. Typically, you go to a club because you align yourself with the social structures of that club and what it promotes. For example, why do we choose one health club over another, or one nightclub instead of another?

Despite not necessitating a physical space, clubs nevertheless need to create a strong identity – and this is the key to their success. Design is at the heart of this identity, and in a culture of consumption where lifestyle tells all, the design needs to build on the social aspirations of its members.

The vast number of clubs on offer means that consumers now have choice, and good design that understands its users will guide that choice. When it comes to built form, the design needs to be so good that the member will see the club as a destination, as a place to experience in its own right.

The clubs in this issue of ⅅ span a wide range of activities, aspirations and identities. From gay clubs in New York to the branded health clubs of London, nightclubs, golf clubs, gentleman's clubs, travel clubs and more, the importance of design is ever present in shaping their identities. ⅅ

The Health
of the Nation

As the British public aspires to current notions of health, beauty and fitness, a whole new industry of dedicated health clubs compete with their interior architecture to attract custom and ultimately membership. **Eleanor Curtis** examines this phenomenon and looks specifically at three trailblazing London clubs, as well as some European examples by ORMS for Holmes Place.

The aerobics fad of the 1980s that successfully crossed the Atlantic from the US to Europe, and introduced us to those snappy concepts such as 'keep fit', 'work out' and 'feel the burn', provided the backbone for what is now a well-established health and fitness industry. In the early days, aerobics classes tended to take place at the local council's sports clubs or a local church hall, the former being open to the whole family. However, in the early 1990s the health club industry took off when private companies entered the market.

According to the International Health, Racquet and Sportsclub Association (IHRSA), the number of private UK clubs and their revenues more than doubled between 1996 and 2001.[1] High streets in the UK's cities and major towns are now littered with named brands of health clubs such as LA Fitness, Canons, Holmes Place and David Lloyd. Emphasis has now shifted away from the state-based 'health of the nation' to a society that values individual gratification and consumption sold, in privately run venues, through the image of personal improvement and beauty.

Boom and Bust

The reason for the boom in health clubs is multilayered and complex. Today people put more time and money into looking after their bodies than was the case 20 or 30 years ago. This might be related to our becoming a generally more health-consciousness society (newspapers and magazines are filled to the brim with articles about good health and food),

or to the general rise in the wealth of our nations that allows us more time for ourselves. Even more so, it may have something to do with modern society's all-pervasive notion of 'body beautiful', which lures us to the gym with the idea of reaching our perfect bodily state.

Whatever the reason, which hints at being less about health and more about aesthetics, the boom has also stimulated a culture of competing interior architecture in which to house these growing numbers of health clubs. The club itself has become a place with which one can identify beyond the activities that occur there. Aesthetics now beat the cardiovascular machines for attention in the new modern health club, the space being defined with sleek minimalist materials, beautiful surfaces, coloured windows and temple-like water/spa areas, resulting in 'zones' that talk to the individual.

Cruising

A visit to a health club has become an experience in itself. Simply cruising the corridors and spaces within can be pleasant and sometimes intriguing. Design for health has come a long way from the days of the local council-run gym often situated in a basement, dark and rank with odours of stale sweat.

In fact, it seems that private health clubs have gone so far as to be less about health per se and more and more about the ideals of modern living in the urban environment – about 'lifestyle'. Indeed, Holmes Place plc, a major player in the top-of-the-range UK health clubs market, has actually renamed itself Holmes Place Lifestyle Clubs AG in its new ventures in Germany and Austria (see later).

Health clubs aim to reflect current lifestyle trends in order to 'click' with what they perceive as the identities, or identity ambitions, of potential members. It is now difficult to distinguish whether it is the activities on offer or the club itself – with its emphasis on spatial zones, lighting and logos – that shapes the identity of a particular club. Entering any of the more up-market health clubs in London today feels more akin to entering a hotel lobby. The lobby has become the all-important first space where the client will soak up the ethos of the club through design – architectural and graphical – before even contemplating a work-out. Corridors, walkways and windows now afford small glimpses of what lies beyond; materials are sumptuous, luxurious, enriching; soft music fills the corners and the lighting is subdued. Through design, the emphasis is placed on offering members 'time out' from their daily lives in a luxurious, calm environment, and not on health and fitness.

Location is also vital to the success of a club. To be competitive, health clubs must position themselves at key and accessible points of a city, where their doors

Previous spread
The sleek and transparent entrance to Broadgate Club West, designed by Allford Hall Monaghan Morris in 1997.

EARLY AUTUMN —
FLEECY CLOUDS
SAIL ACROSS T...

Broadgate Club West, London, 1997
Allford Hall Monaghan Morris (AHMM)

Broadgate Club West

Above left
Japanese-style poetry (haikus)
floats on walls, floors, pillars
and glass, with messages of
calm and wellbeing.

Above right
The changing rooms are tiled
dark blue, enhancing the clean
lines and symmetry.

Although already dated in design terms, Broadgate Club West's innovative design retains its powerful statement in health-club culture with its refreshing design concept, which focuses on leisure and luxury without compromising high-quality specifications.

The Regent's Place site in central London was conceived as a sister club to the highly successful London City based Broadgate Club that opened in 1989. The identity of the club and how it could meet the aspirations of its target membership group (defined as time-poor, highly affluent professionals in their late 20s and upwards) had an enormous impact on the design issues.

'We always knew we wanted to create a health club that would make a break from the traditional stereotype of the sweat-box gym,' says Paul Monaghan of AHMM. 'When you walk into the entrance hall, it feels like a luxurious hotel, evoking a similar feel to that of Ian Schrager's St Martin's Lane Hotel, for instance.

'I think it was a natural follow-on from the boom that occurred in the restaurant and club industries during the late 1980s. And as a result, design became more important [to health clubs].'

Fees are high and so, naturally, are members' expectations. AHMM was under no illusion about the importance of attention to detail. The changing rooms are tiled navy blue creating an ambience one might find at a more traditional gentleman's club, whereas the gym space is defined as urban and contemporary, punctuated with colours

and texts. The club also houses a restaurant, with furniture designed by Andrew Stafford. 'We wanted to create a luxurious space, not for passing through in haste, but somewhere members could relax and that would be comparative to other genre restaurants our members visit.'

The interior of the club is embraced by a glazed back-lit 'Blue Wall', a feature that was inspired by the sister club's blue tile mural by Howard Hodgkin. As Monaghan asserts: 'Although more Rothko than Hodgkin, the wall articulates the two spatial requirements demanded by the brief; on the one hand open-plan areas for the gym and bar, and on the other the cellular rooms for the offices, changing rooms and the Charles Worthington Hair Salon.'

The luminous blue wall adds an aquatic feel to the interior – an irony considering the facility lacks a swimming pool (due to structural restrictions). The innovative lighting strategies, where light bounces off surfaces and walls shimmer, have combated the common diagnosis of 'gym fatigue' and are instead mood enhancing. The colour of the light changes from deep blue to purple over the course of the day, not unlike an artificial sky.

The architects have purveyed this interest throughout Broadgate Club West, collaborating with graphic designers Studio Myerscough to ensure marketing literature, graphics and signage are fully integrated with the architecture. The use of haikus (Japanese three-part poems) on walls, floors, pillars and glass, as well as in the marketing literature, providing messages of calm and wellbeing, strongly emphasise the club's interest in holistic care and are intended by the architects to help alleviate people's anxiety of gyms, and ultimately change their perceptions of exercise from chore to pleasure.

Although initially developed by Broadgate plc, the club changed hands in 1998 and is now owned by Holmes Place plc.

can open to greet workers on their way home. One club, located in London's Soho, has named itself the Third Space to denote its place in the individual's life – beyond home (the first space) and work (the second) (see later). However, a central location in a built-up urban area usually means adapting an existing space, often presenting a design challenge for architects.

Chill-Out Zones

As the role of the health club has become less about health and more about the modern lifestyle of the individual, the use of space has evolved to match. The main focus of the health club was once the gym area, sold on its merits in offering the latest machine technology. Today, however, the gym area, typified by row

buying up everywhere in the city and using a formula for interior architecture that is becoming predictable – albeit predictably cool, calm and sleek. It is fair to say that branding has its advantages – a name can be associated with certain levels of service and standards, the customs are familiar and safe, and clients know they are buying into a particular identity. However, could the interior architecture of health clubs not be a little more daring, rather than reproducing another hotel lobby culture couched within health and fitness slogans? What would a health club that pushed the boundaries of health zones a little further look like?

The case studies presented here outline a number of different approaches to the design of health clubs in the city, from branding to the very unique. They include three very different clubs in central London – the

The main focus of the health club was once the gym area, sold on its merits in offering the latest machine technology. Today, however, the gym area, typified by row upon row of machines, often in an uninspiring space, is just one element of the club. Contemporary city health clubs have arranged their total floor areas in a more 'holistic' way.

upon row of machines, often in an uninspiring space, is just one element of the club. Contemporary city health clubs have arranged their total floor areas in a more 'holistic' way. The water area (referred to as the 'wet area' by architects) is now a combination of sauna, Jacuzzi, steam room and swimming pool, with a pool deck for relaxation. The dry areas include studios for spin, tone and pump (and other fitness classes), studios for yoga and changing rooms. And social areas include the reception, cafés, bars and sometimes restaurants. Other areas might include relaxation rooms or temples with soft music, dim lights and fish tanks, treatment and beauty-therapy rooms and hairdressing salons.

A pattern is emerging regarding the design of these up-market health clubs as architects tailor spaces to match the projected needs of club members. Health clubs are now cool spaces within which to chill out from daily life. But has design become diluted as the formula is branded? The big names in health clubs are

Broadgate Club West, Regent's Place, by Allford Hall Monaghan Morris; Canary Riverside, Canary Wharf, by Walters & Cohen; and the Third Space, Soho, by Richard Hywell Evans/ Collcutt & Hamp – with the final study introducing the work of architects ORMS for Holmes Place plc in the UK, Germany and Austria.

The studies show, for example, how the graphic-design team at Allford Hall Monaghan Morris enhanced the notion of calm and well-being at the sumptuously designed Broadgate Club West, and how the emphasis was placed on ultimate luxury at the Canary Riverside, by Walters & Cohen, to match the expectations of the hotel of which it is a part. They also demonstrate how the Third Space club has deliberately tried to move away from the notion of club design branding, creating its own identity in its name, use of graphics, open use of space and the unusual vertical axis to its site plan. Lastly, the results of the branding of Holmes Place plc by architects ORMS at a variety of very different European sites raises the question of whether the site itself can provoke radically alternative design solutions despite the branding brief from the client.

Canary Riverside Health Club, London, 2000
Walters & Cohen

The Canary Riverside Health Club was commissioned by Holmes Place plc. This four-storey health club and spa, situated in the Four Seasons Hotel at Canary Wharf, was flagged to be the most luxurious of all health clubs to match the expectations and standards of the internationally renowned hotel. Indeed, the materials are exquisite and the spaces radiate luxury and leisure. The pool is walled with green granite and the changing rooms are lined with timber. With views out over the River Thames, the health club is the ultimate luxury health club and spa in an urban environment.

Walters & Cohen has a history of design for Holmes Place, ranging from lower down the scale right through to the top of the range in luxury. The architects were approached by Holmes Place in 1995 regarding smaller-scale work at its branch in Hammersmith, and later to refurbish its flagship club on the Fulham Road in Chelsea. In 1996 Holmes Place asked Walters & Cohen to adapt an old public building in Wood Green, north London, on a restricted budget, for an 'affordable health club', otherwise known as Holmes Place Fitness. In 1997 the architects designed a further health club for Holmes Place in a disused supermarket building.

Canary Riverside, however, was a shell when it was handed over to the architects for design. The brief was clear, modern design to maximise the existing space. The design philosophy from the outset was to use a palette of the highest-quality natural materials whilst maximising the water theme and views of the River Thames.

The area set aside for the club and pool is arranged over four floors in a new complex designed by, among others, Philippe Starck and Koetter Kim Associates. The pool hall on floor 2 has full-height glazing on both sides with views over the river and the landscaped garden. The reception is divided over two levels with the clubroom and bar situated at the lower level. The gym occupies the upper two floors of the club, which have breathtaking views over London and the river. The luxurious spa is on the lowest level, one level below the pool and main reception area, at the same level as the river walk. Natural light is drawn into the lower level through large openings in the existing shell, enhanced by the open staircase with glass balustrades.

Materials are hard-wearing but beautiful, robust yet elegant. Walters & Cohen has used green granite in the spa, timber in the reception, and steel and glass for the staircase. The emphasis has been on luxury, fitting with the standards of Four Seasons Hotel visitors who will predictably use the health club, along with nearby office workers.

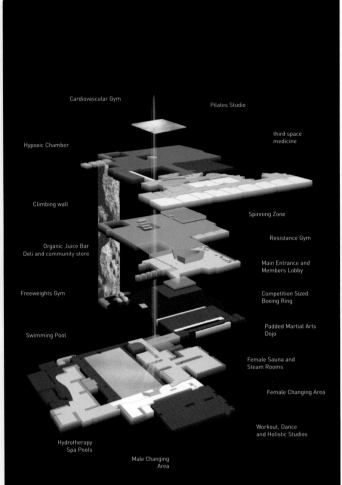

Cardiovascular Gym

Pilates Studio

Hypoxic Chamber

third space
medicine

Climbing wall

Spinning Zone

Resistance Gym

Organic Juice Bar
Deli and community store

Main Entrance and
Members Lobby

Competition Sized
Boxing Ring

Freeweights Gym

Padded Martial Arts
Dojo

Female Sauna and
Steam Rooms

Swimming Pool

Female Changing Area

Workout, Dance
and Holistic Studios

Hydrotherapy
Spa Pools

Male Changing
Area

The Third Space, London, 2001
Collcutt and Hamp

The Third Space

Opposite
All zones look on to and
into other zones, as the
pool does to the studio.

Above left
This dramatic view of the
pool reveals the open,
vertical axis to the club
and its use of industrial
elements in the design.

Above right
Section through the club.

While Broadgate Club West is about luxury and modern design, and Canary Riverside luxury and water, the Third Space is a completely different and distinguishable type of health club. Situated in London's Soho, the club promotes the idea of the health club as one's third space after home and work. It attempts to disperse with the concept of an exclusive membership by offering this third space as open for individual interpretation. This is apparent right down to the graphic design, whereby the corporate and ID cards have three circles, the first two in different shades of green and the third left blank in order that it can be 'filled' with whatever idea one wishes.

'Perhaps the concept of the Third Space was to dispel the concept of membership as a clique. Third Space could be used as members liked, they didn't have to conform to any set of rules,' comments Nick Farnell of architects Collcutt and Hamp, who designed the club.

The client – Longshot Health & Fitness Ltd, headed by Oliver Vigors, a veteran of London's restaurant and club culture – wanted to create a 'different gym' that was more along the lines of the clubs, bars and restaurants industry than sitting alongside brand-name health clubs – hence the live DJ who mixes the music for the aerobics and spinning classes, the live gospel choir on a Sunday and the Prada make-up launch that was held here.

The entire club is spread over three-and-a-half floors, totalling some 40,000 square feet, and includes links to various retail units such as the organic food store Fesh & Wild and a massage store, Relax. The top floor of the building is a fully integrated, noninterventional medical facility with alternative practitioners, dieticians and physiotherapists.

The space is divided into three zones, with each space interconnected via glass walls and glass floors. The only room not visually accessible is the pilates/yoga studio. The Hypoxic chamber (sealed off for high-altitude training) is enclosed with a glass floor and walls, extending even further the feeling of space and height. The entrance space directs the vista to the interior of the club where each floor, including the 20-metre ozone-treated swimming pool, is visible. The three gymnasiums – cardiovascular, resistance and spinning, and hard-core – are stacked one above the other, the latter situated on the mezzanine, which is accessed via a 'catwalk'.

'The materials used were chosen for their robustness, such as concrete, glass and galvanised and stainless steel, and avoided the typical "blonde-wood look" found in so many health clubs,' says Farnell. 'Besides gazing at themselves, members can also see all the different elements of the club as they work out. This encourages participation and makes people less intimidated to try other equipment or activities.'

Interestingly, Collcutt and Hamp also contributed to the overall graphics for the club. Collcutt & Hamp New Media for the Third Space provided a mixture of photography and digital artwork to create a custom set of icons for defining each zone. A video installation in the lobby area, driven by custom software, displays randomly generated animations 'reflecting the nature of the Third Space'.

Above
Shellmex health club, London.
The wet zone, with swimming
pool and Jacuzzi, is located on
the lower level with the
clubroom and café at the
mezzanine level, offering a
spectators' gallery to the pool
area. The extended use of
colour enhances an otherwise
unlit space.

In London, ORMS went on to refurbish the early
20th-century listed building the Shellmex House
for one of Holmes Place's most centrally located
clubs. The building itself imposed various
limitations — it had no natural light and was
sandwiched between other buildings — which
dictated the use of space.

Above, top
Kaiserwasser health club,
Vienna. The pool at dusk with
spectacular views overlooking
the city.

Above, bottom
The Kaisserwasser building
was originally an office block.
While retaining its facade, ORMS
has made use of colour for
distinction and discretion (for
the changing rooms).

London-based architects ORMS have been working with Holmes Place
plc for the last five years. Their first project for a health club was the
Ibex House in the City, whereby the basement of this landmark
building was completely rekitted out. The technical challenges of the
project were broad and included archaeological and drainage issues.
The club was taken on by Holmes Place plc in 1998, establishing a
relationship between ORMS and the health club company from which
followed a series of commissions for the adaptive reuse of centrally
located buildings for the company's top-of-the-range health clubs.

In London, ORMS went on to refurbish the early 20th-century listed
building the Shellmex House, on The Strand, for one of Holmes
Place's most centrally located clubs. The building itself imposed
various limitations – it had no natural light and was sandwiched
between other buildings – which dictated the use of space.

The club, which opened in 2002, is arranged on three floors of
the building from the Strand entrance level downwards, with the
swimming pool occupying a double-height space that can be viewed
from the clubroom. The changing rooms, along with other spaces, are
located beneath and adjacent to the pool at the Embankment level of
the building (level with the River Thames). The design takes members
down into the heart of the building, offering views that link the
internal spaces, bringing together all the elements of the club.

In addition, ORMS is currently working on another central London
health club for Holmes Place in a prime piece of real estate on Oxford
Street, a site that once housed the clothes retailer C&A. Again, this is
a challenging location, in the heart of retail land, that is imposing
serious technical issues regarding water facilities and air circulation.

'Location is the key to the success of Holmes Place,' says Oliver
Richards of ORMS. 'The spaces they give us are typically problem spaces
but centrally located. These are known as "drop-in" clubs in the city and
are tailored towards more modern, urban living. Their other clubs
outside the city are known as "destination clubs" – the club itself being
the destination. These generate two very different sorts of design briefs.'

Holmes Place had seen the potential saturation of the health-
club market in the UK and was keen to be one of the first to establish
its name throughout the country as a brand offering quality clubs
with the emphasis on luxury and lifestyle. The company also saw
potential in mainland Europe, where the concept of health clubs was
relatively immature, and brought in ORMS to design its first turnkey
project in Vienna, which was completed in 1998. The club, which
responded in design terms to the local culture, was to act as a
template for other central European projects in Germany and
Austria. (Holmes Place now has more than 230,000 members in
over 60 health clubs spread across Greater London and southeast
England, with 15 clubs opening in Europe.)

The club at Kaiserwasser in Vienna is split over a number of
levels. The public areas – the foyer, clubroom and crêche – are
arranged on the ground floor, with the gym, studios and changing
rooms on the second and, unusually, the pool hall and spa on the

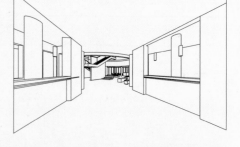

Above
Provinzialplatz health
club, Düsseldorf.
Sketch of a diver as
seen through the 2-
metre fish-eye lens at
the bottom of the pool,
housed in the ceiling
above the reception.

Right
Gendarmenmarkt
health club, Berlin.
A swimmer looking out
on to the turnstiles
in the reception area.

Opposite, top
Börseplatz health club,
Vienna. The glass-and-
steel open staircase,
bathed in blue light,
gives access to all
zones.

Opposite, middle
Börseplatz health club,
Vienna. The dramatic
reception area reveals
the blue-lit atrium
behind.

Opposite, bottom
Gendarmenmarkt
health club, Berlin.
View into the clubroom
through the glass
wall inscribed with
the word 'beauty'.

Note
1 'The New Puritans: Working Out is Painful and Boring. So Why Bother?', *The Economist*, 19 December 2002.

rooftop level, affording spectacular views across Vienna and its landmark St Stefan's Cathedral. The water and spa area at the top was seen as the club's 'jewel in the crown', designed as a glass pavilion with extensive views over the city.

Working in different local cultures to that of the UK, and London, ORMS identified significant disparities that dictated their designs for the central European clubs. The notion of the spa, for example, has a long history in central Europe, where people would spend days and weekends relaxing at these resorts. Issues of nudity are also much more liberal than in the UK; for example, both sexes are more used to sharing steam and sauna rooms and casually strolling around in a pair of flip-flops and nothing else. As a result, much more emphasis has been placed on the spa and water areas in the Austrian and German clubs, with perhaps four different types of saunas, six different types of showers and more social areas in the water zones.

'Holmes Place are trying to create a club [in central Europe] that can respond to modern needs on a social level. It is not a fitness or health club. In fact, the whole term "health club" in German has a very negative connotation and denotes more of a sanatorium or convalescence home. Holmes Place have renamed themselves Holmes Place Lifestyle Clubs AG in Germany and Austria to suit the local culture', comments Sean Hatcher of ORMS.

He continues: 'The social aspects to the club – like cafés and restaurants – are very important here in Germany and Austria, as is the water area with its relaxing zones. Members will come and spend the whole day in the water area as opposed to just dropping in for a swim.'

The firm's work for Holmes Place's second club in Vienna, the Börseplatz club, was to a very different brief: to 'provide a sophisticated and exclusive environment balanced within the energetic atmosphere of a health club' at a location on the outskirts of the city. The passage into the club is via an original marble cupola, retained for planning reasons, to a modern raft ceiling that features the reception desk and foyer. The naturally lit, 18-foot atrium above connects all of the club's facilities by a series of stairs and walkways. Glass vision slots offer angled views to the enveloping gyms and studios beyond. The pool hall and spa are located within the lower levels, with an illuminated glass wall that provides visual focus and uniformity to a space split between Jacuzzi, pool and relaxation.

The ORMS design in Germany for a Holmes Place Lifestyle Club in Friedrichstrasse, Berlin, the Gendarmenmarkt club represents a new generation of lifestyle clubs. It is situated over three floors with striking views across the city throughout the interiors. The entrance is dominated by a slice of the pool – a window cut into the dividing wall between the pool and the foyer. Within the pool hall itself is a light installation, or 'mood wall that divides the pool area from the relaxation space', offering 'an oasis of calm within the fast tempo of Berlin's city centre'. The gym is positioned on the first floor and has natural daylight (unusual for gym areas) provided by rooflights. The clubroom is immediately above the main foyer and at the entrance to the gym, acting as the social heart of the club with cafés, dining and lounging areas.

Similarly, the Am Gürzenisch club in Cologne, which is still under construction, is being designed to create a sense of intrigue and mystery by affording glimpses into rooms and zones from the walkways and shared areas. For example, the reception is dominated by a slice of the pool, at water level, through a window. In turn, this window acts as a mirror on the other side, giving swimmers the impression that the pool is twice its length.

But it is the new Holmes Place Provinzialplatz health club in Düsseldorf that is perhaps the most exciting in terms of design. Though work is still in progress, ORMS is adapting the building to house the club whilst maintaining its rounded egg-shape. The pool will be situated above the reception, and a huge 2-metre-radius glass lens will sit at the bottom of the pool and in the ceiling of the reception, so that members will have a slightly distorted view of the swimmers above. ⊿

The three London health clubs were researched by Lizzie Meadows.

Japanese Golf Club Culture

Entertaining with Exclusivity

Since the middle of the 20th century, golf clubs in Japan have developed their own distinctive culture centred on entertainment of business clients rather than on social interaction. **Masaaki Takahashi** describes the history of golf in Japan and how some clubs in Japan and Southern Korea are leading the way by creating more modern

Golf clubs in Japan have a club culture quite distinct from those in the US or UK. This is largely due to a very different cultural interpretation of what constitutes a club. The word 'club', or 'kurabu', was introduced into Japanese during the late 19th century and was denoted by kanji (Chinese characters) meaning 'group of people to share enjoyment'. This etymology partly explains why for the Japanese the word club does not generally refer to places or activities that are members only. A few clubs, in the Western sense, were founded in the 19th century among the upper classes to bring people together for a particular academic or commercial purpose, but it was the Japanese notion of the club aimed at enjoyment rather than social exchange that caught on in mainstream culture. These 'clubs' brought people together for the explicit purpose of entertainment – eating, drinking, singing, dancing by geisha, fireworks and exhibitions. According to architectural historian Shinya Hashizume in *Clubs and the Japanese*, the two types of club culture bifurcated sometime between 1887 and 1897. [1] It is a dichotomy that has remained until the present day, with golf clubs belonging firmly to the popular Japanese club tradition.

It was only with the opening of the Rokumeikan in Tokyo in 1883 that the Japanese upper classes were exposed to the reality of the social world of clubs in the original sense. Rokumeikan was an elitist club designed by Josiah Conder for the Japanese to entertain foreign diplomats and dignitaries. A potent symbol of Westernisation, it was built under the aegis of the Minister of Foreign Affairs, Kaoru Inoue, with the explicit intention of creating the correct social environment for improving foreign relations, so that the inequalities of the European and American devised trade agreements could be readdressed.

Later in the postwar years, the Japanese became smitten with the foreign sport of golf, and golf courses proliferated all over the archipelago. However, if outwardly golf appeared to be a Western import, it was the indigenous Japanese notion of 'the club' that flourished through golf clubs. With almost entirely male memberships, golf clubs became the perfect venues for business entertainment. If, however, the function of the golf clubhouses as places of corporate entertainment aided their rise in the boom years, when the economic bubble burst in the 1990s it also contributed to their decline. In order to survive, golf clubs have come to realise that they must attract a wider membership – both in terms of age and gender. This requires a radical rethinking of golf club culture regarding club identity and the way that a broader membership might be catered for through a club's spaces and facilities. By firstly charting the history of golf in Japan and the exclusivity previously inherent in the sport, this article will explore golf clubs' relation to design and new directions for design strategies. The potential way forward will be examined through a short discussion of golf in South Korea and three case studies of golf clubs that all exhibit a clear design vision through their architecture.

Previous spread
Public clubhouse of PINX Golf
Club, Cheju-do, Korea, 1999
Architect Jun Itami

Opposite
Night view, Taco Golf Club,
Chiba prefecture, Japan.
Interior redecoration by Hijyun
Kasuya, 1999.

Above left
A drab eatery at the Taco Golf
Club has been converted into a
cosy restaurant. Interior
designer Hijyun Kasuya.

Above right
Bathroom renovation, Sebe
Ballesteros Golf Club, Ibaraki
prefecture, Japan, 1997.
Interior designer Hijyun
Kasuya.

Above right, inset
The bleak bathroom of the
Sebe Ballesteros Golf Club
prior to renovation.

There are some 2,400 golf courses in Japan, which almost matches the total number in the UK. Their area surpasses that of the metropolis of Tokyo (216,626 square metres). The player population stands at approximately 9.6 million, and the cumulative total of golf club visitors is approximately 84 million per year. The gross annual income of golf courses is about 1.25 trillion yen. These figures indicate the enormous popularity of the sport in Japan, and the fact there is an overwhelming number of golf courses in the country. However, as the construction of courses often leads to the destruction of the natural environment, and because maintenance requires the use of pesticides and herbicides, perceptions of golf courses are not always positive, and citizens' movements against their construction are common.

The history of golf in Japan began in 1901 when British trading merchant Arthur H Gloom opened the first course on the Rokko mountains in Kobe. Initially, the course had only four holes but later developed into the Kobe Golf Club with nine holes. The members were all Westerners and kimono-clad boys in bamboo sheath sandals caddied – it was definitely a very colonial set-up. The first golf course for Japanese was the Tokyo Golf Course, which opened in 1913 and was followed by a myriad of courses across the country as well as in Manchukuo and the colonies of Korea and Taiwan.

Defeat during the Second World War brought golf to the verge of extinction in Japan, but in 1957 the country won the pair and individual games in the fifth World Cup of Golf held in Tokyo, appealing to nationalism and creating a golf boom. Prior to the war, golf had mostly been the sport of the upper classes. However, postwar it penetrated the social strata to include ordinary, and especially business, people due to its adoption as a tool for client entertainment along with mahjong.

Quite specific to Japan is the multitude of practice ranges. The obsession with the brushing up of golf skills spills over into everyday life, where men in dark suits can often be seen practising their swing with an umbrella on railway station platforms. Golf clubs soon became investments, and the cost of membership soared during the bubble economy. By 1992 the total number of golf course visitors reached a record high of over 100 million per year. After that, however, visitors and turnovers continued to decline in parallel with the worsening Japanese economy. Since about 2000, deficits and bankruptcies have been especially serious despite the increasing number of courses.

History tells us that sport has predominantly centred around the male body. Women were previously excluded, even from public events such as the Olympic Games, and their social marginality prevented them from enjoying sports. This inherent exclusiveness is doubled in the case of clubs and their cultures. Unlike the French salons, where women have always played a central role, English clubs were generally closed to the opposite sex. Golf is one of the most male-centred sports, with a multitude of chauvinistic anecdotes even today. Many golf clubs have stipulations that reveal their reluctance to have female members, and there are still a few players who regard golf clubs as liberty halls for men.

The majority of Japanese golf clubhouses are built for businessmen to entertain their clients. Naturally their designs are male-oriented. Females account for only 9 per cent of the clientele and facilities for them are of merely secondary consideration. For example, women's changing rooms and washrooms are often placed in an inconvenient location towards the back of the clubhouse and are disproportionately small. And their bathrooms and shower rooms are usually bleakly designed, in contrast to those for men. Also common are banal, stereotypical furniture and family-restaurant-like bare dining

designs, has got rid of any of the flashiness and conservatism of golf club culture and intentionally created stylish corporate identities and interiors.

In modern society, the visual representation of sport – whether through body images or evocations of aspirational lifestyles – has become a potent tool for sports-related industries. In terms of image consumption, golf offers an important element – the club. Although elsewhere in the world golf clubs place a great deal of emphasis on the amenities they can offer to individuals as members and the society this affords, in Japan the reverse is true. There is little club spirit to be enjoyed through being a member of a golf club, which goes some way to explaining exactly why the facilities are so poor.

In terms of administration, Japanese golf clubs fall into three categories: public interest corporations, joint-stock companies and 'deposit membership' organisations. The last accounts for about 80 per cent of all clubs; each

Whereas it was previously desirable to adopt the decor of the traditional British club to evoke a prestigious atmosphere, it has now become much more common to refurbish clubhouse interiors in a simpler style. In order to attract young people it is necessary for the ambience of clubs to become more informal. Just as in fashion, the trend in golf-related design is now towards the casual.

halls with a poor menu. Women are a frivolous distraction, very much on the sidelines of traditional male golf culture.

The interior designer Hijyun Kasuya is a golfer who has used her experiences of the sport to inform two recent projects to renovate public clubhouses in a more informal manner. Whereas it was previously desirable to adopt the decor, emblems and paraphernalia of the traditional British club to evoke a prestigious atmosphere, it has now become much more common to refurbish clubhouse interiors in a simpler style. In order to attract young people it is necessary for the ambience of clubs to become more informal. Just as in fashion, the trend in golf-related design is now towards the casual. Among the young, especially young women, golf has been regarded for many years as synonymous with the outdated, middle-aged and frumpy. To reverse this situation and attract female golfers, Kasuya, in her

club is a private organisation, the members of which pay a deposit to obtain membership. This membership is sometimes traded at an exorbitant price, and as a result has even triggered cases of fraud or fraudulent schemes. Requirements for admission to prestigious golf courses are extremely strict and rumour has it that one such club even declined the incumbent and former prime ministers' applications at the same time!

But prestige should not be everything. The relaxation and social opportunities a club can offer should be more important, though these appear to be the very things that are lacking in Japanese clubs, where it seems the members' rooms are in fact rarely utilised. So why has golf become a tool of entertainment for business despite the poor social amenities provided by the sport's clubhouses? In answer to this question, in Japan the function of business entertainment is not to establish friendly ties between a businessperson and his or her client. Instead it gives the client a personal benefit (enjoyment of the game in the case of golf) in

PINX Golf Club, Cheju-Do prefecture, Korea, 1999
Architect Jun Itami

PINX Golf Club, Cheju-do
prefecture, Korea, 1999

Opposite and above
Exterior and entrance hall of
the members' clubhouse.
Columns in the hall resemble
traditional Korean stone towers.

Right and inset
Exterior and entrance hall of
the public clubhouse. The
ceiling of the hall uses
Japanised oak.

The members' and public clubhouses for the PINX Golf Club on Cheju-do, Korea's largest island, which lies halfway between Korea and Japan in the East China Sea, were designed by Jun Itami. Known as the Korean Hawaii for its warm climate, the island has Korea's third highest mountain (Halla-san, at 1,950 metres) and many other beautiful tourist spots.

The members' clubhouse has a total floor area of 3616.90 square metres, and the public clubhouse an area of 641.57 square metres. The owner and architect honed the theme 'Harmony with Nature and Resonance with Mother Earth' for both projects. The public clubhouse sits at the top of a small hill. The members' clubhouse is at the foot of the hill. A road separates the two. Half buried in the ground, the former is built in harmony with the horizon and the edges of the surrounding mountains. To minimise the effects of local gales from the northwest, its long axis line is placed in the same direction. Itami believes that architects need to study traditional local culture and make the most of it in their works, and that this eventually leads to the creation of something international. His work in Cheju-do is a very relaxing space with a Korean flavour, with only a hint of Japanese tastes. As to the layouts of the two buildings, the architect's intention was to make them gender-equal. In fact, although they are very authentic they contain no traffic lines that are inconvenient for women. At completion, this golf club was ranked the second in Korea by US magazine *Golf Digest* and influenced others that followed. It is still one of the most popular clubs in the country and there are a number of imperfect imitators nearby.

However, with a new crop of young talent completing their education in the West, the Korean architectural world has moved on from its period of copying, and some argue that Itami has influenced this process. Exclusivity is inevitable to maintain high quality and, rather than being critical of this, Itami seems to be more interested in creating golf courses in his own style that go hand in hand with the local climate.

A-One Country Club, Yangsan-shi, Korea, 1997

Above
One of three pavilions for resting and taking refreshments.

Opposite, main picture
Interior shot of the main lounge.

Opposite, inset
Detail of north facade showing the limestone, lead-coated copper roofs and clear glass that formed the palette for the building.

Notes
1 Shinya Hashizume, *Clubs and the Japanese*, Gakugei-shuppen (Tokyo), 1989.
2 Norbert Elias and Eric Dunning, *Quest for Excitement*, Blackwell Publishers (Oxford), 1986; and Eric Dunning and Kenneth Sheard, *Barbarians, Gentlemen and Players: A Sociological Study of the Development of Rugby Football*, New York University Press (New York), 1979.

exchange for granting a favour that puts the host ahead of competitors.

With Japan in the midst of an economic slump, golf is now in decline. The most promising direction for the future of golf clubs lies in greater openness, and a broader membership that extends to women, younger people and those of retirement age. Clubs have a fertile market among the older generation and must cater for them in terms of their organisation and design. Golf clubs are, however, only just beginning to understand that they require new members beyond their tried and tested customers – expense-account businesspeople. The emergence of a new social golf culture is thus essential for the survival of golf clubs. Fresh design is an important catalyst that can both draw people in and make golf clubs places where people want to be and where they can mix socially.

Golf in Japan should perhaps take its impetus from South Korea, which has had a distinguished performance in recent international competitions and is full of potential. There are 158 clubs in the country, 114 of which were members-only and 44 public at the time of writing. The golf population is approximately 1.5 million, about 16 per cent of that of Japan. Golf is gaining greater popularity among South Koreans, and each year increasing numbers of young people are taking up the game. However,

Kazuya Suzuki, chief editor of *Golf-jo Seminar* magazine, says it is enjoyed mostly by the rich, as was the case in prewar Japan. In 2002 the numbers of golf course visitors topped 10 million for the first time, meaning that, on average, each course is visited by 63,000 golfers annually. There are more than a dozen courses for which membership is currently on sale, costing anything upwards of 200 million Korean won (around US$169,000). Worth special mention is the Benest Golf Club (27 holes), which sells second-time membership for 550 million Korean won (approximately US$466,000). It seems golf is still an exclusive leisure activity in South Korea.

Many sports, such as golf, tennis and football were developed in their modern form in 19th-century Britain, which successfully exported them throughout the British Empire and its extensive trade network. In Victorian England, sport became a successful tool for social and physical control, as expounded by Norbert Elias, Eric Dunning and Kenneth Sheard.[2] According to these authors, modern sports have their origins partly in the tense relations between social classes in Britain and the conflict between amateurs and professionals generated by the rise of the bourgeoisie after the Industrial Revolution, and partly in an education system that had its emphasis on masculinity and gentlemanliness. In this age of anti-cultural colonialism and anti-chauvinism, and changing social classes, club sports will transform. Perhaps the clue to this transformation is to be found in the way the game is enjoyed in non-Western or post-colonial countries. ⌂

Designed by LA-based up-and-coming John Friedman Alice Kimm Architects and SAC International, owned by Kimm's father, this clubhouse in Yangsan-shi, Korea, has the atmosphere of an art museum with a beautiful garden. The first floor houses the owner's VIP guest suites and a series of private dining rooms accessed via a long, skylit hallway.

Kimm regards golf in Korea, unlike in the US, as a sport for the upper and middle classes only. Though it is indeed the case that even in America the game is not open to everyone, when compared with the situation in Asia it is certainly far less exclusive. This exclusivity is evident in the Korean project's form. The clubhouse sits in the centre of the course, making it a focal point. The architect's initial idea was for a building with a series of roofs terracing down into the ground,

so that it would 'melt' into the earth. However, the client stated firmly that the building should be more monumental in stature, to appeal to the members of this 'exclusive' club. The solution was to use monolithic stone volumes that anchor the building to the earth, while using lots of glass and eaves to allow the space a certain lightness. The roofs were given a butterfly shape, tilting upwards to satisfy the owner's desire for monumentality, yet floating above the volumes, their forms making reference to the mountains beyond.

According to Kimm: 'We have found that the open, fluid, dynamic spaces of modern contemporary architecture appeal very much to people of all cultures, ages and so on. I expect that the groups of people who come to Yangsan to play golf lead a generally active and athletic lifestyle, which furthers their attraction to the open, airy, light-filled spaces of the golf club.'

Lakewood Golf Club, Tomioka clubhouse,
Tomioka City, Gunma prefecture, Japan, 1996
Architect: Kengo Kuma

Lakewood Golf Club, Tomioka
clubhouse, Tomioka City,
Japan, 1996

Opposite
Exterior of Tomioka clubhouse,
showing its impressive
aluminium louvres and
cantilever structure. Water and
rocks sing a homage to Frank
Lloyd Wright.

Above right
Furniture in Kuma's original
design.

Right
The reflecting pool creates a
light and bright atmosphere.

Designed by Kengo Kuma, one of the most active architects in Japan,
this clubhouse, with a total floor area of 8,187 square metres, is
characterised by a sense of lightness and transparency, a reflection of
the architect's emphasis on materials and inspiration from Frank Lloyd
Wright. Plentiful sunlight merges the inside and outside of the building,
producing a sense of spaciousness.

From the entrance, visitors can see straight through the
transparent entrance hall on to the course. Inside, two halls act as a
dual centre for the traffic lines. On the right of the entrance hall are
the reception and a shop, and on the left a lounge, restaurant and
conference room. Stairs at the end of the hall lead down to the ground
floor where another hall has a locker room to its left, a caddie
master's room and a starting terrace on the right. Traffic lines from
these two halls flow smoothly.

'Today people want places they visit to be a comfortable extension of
their own home,' says Kuma. 'Golf clubs are no exception. But exactly
what makes them feel at home? They don't like anything decorative.
They want to feel nature through light and water. In this golf club you
can sense nature close to you, even inside the building. I wanted to wipe
out the usual image of clubs with subdued lighting.'

Believing that people are more able to relax in neutral surroundings,
Kuma avoided adopting local colours, in interesting contrast to Itami. On
exclusivity, he says: 'The exclusivity in the European sense takes the
form of thick walls which define separate spaces. But in Japan,
traditionally buildings have a wooden frame and are not suitable for
such thick walls. Instead we create exclusivity by the use of floors. For
example, the moment you step on a tatami-matted floor that is raised
just a step, you feel something different than when on the lower floor. I
wanted to get this type of exclusivity into iron and glass shape in this
clubhouse. With minimal walls, the building is designed to give a sense
of detachment from this mortal coil the moment you step out of your
car. In general I think clubhouses will go casual.' He continues: 'It might
be interesting, for instance, to create one with only a roof and no walls,
not even glass ones. You know the splendid Katsura Detached Palace in
Kyoto doesn't utilise glass either.'

Come Out, Join In, Get Off

Gay Clubs in Chelsea, New York

David Sokol describes how gay men are redefining queer architecture in the club spaces of New York's Chelsea neighbourhood. The direction, it seems, is assimilation.

New York City's Chelsea neighbourhood encompasses just several dozen square blocks on Manhattan's west side, but is nevertheless the East Coast capital of queer culture. Where Christopher Street, to the south, once drew in every facet of New York's gay community, now it's Seventh and Eighth Avenues in the teens and twenties that is home to, or destination for, Chelsea boys, leather daddies, twinks, str8-acting guys and everything in between.

Indeed, Chelsea's populace, like the American gay community, is fragmented beyond what a typical heterosexual person might believe. And in this vein, Chelsea's club spaces – health clubs, sex clubs and nightclubs – do not lend themselves to a standardised perspective of what defines the space as queer. They are designed to bring people together, to social or salacious ends, and for each purpose or audience they are distinct. Thanks to assimilation, however, they are becoming more narrow and subtle.

Two Principles: Orgasm, Urbanity

According to historian and critic Aaron Betsky, the primary purpose of queer space is orgasm:

It is the space in which your body dissolves into the world and your senses smooth all reality into continuous waves of pleasure … Orgasmic space leaves you vulnerable and happy in that vulnerability, because you are at the center of your experience.[1]

Queer space does not become orgasmic space by bodily ecstasy alone. Betsky's research uncovers numerous variations of orgasmic space, from overly sensuous, object-laden environments to parodies of social spaces (think Oscar Wilde's home and any La Cage revue, respectively). Regardless of its manifestation, orgasmic space defies traditional architectural orders as well as other social boundaries.

Surmounting traditional architecture strictures is one way to represent one's strength in marginalisation. And within the sphere of contemporary Chelsea club-life, themes and variations on this defining principle are

Previous spread
The stylised minimalism of XL frames the activity of patrons of the lounge and bar, on a typical night in Chelsea.

Below
The SBNY dance floor, set up for cocktail hour. The dance floor is sandwiched between video projection screens (rear) and a stage equipped with shower heads (not pictured).

Opposite, top
Looking across the SBNY dance floor, towards the rear bar.

Opposite, bottom
Of SBNY's three bars, the first is just steps from the front entrance.

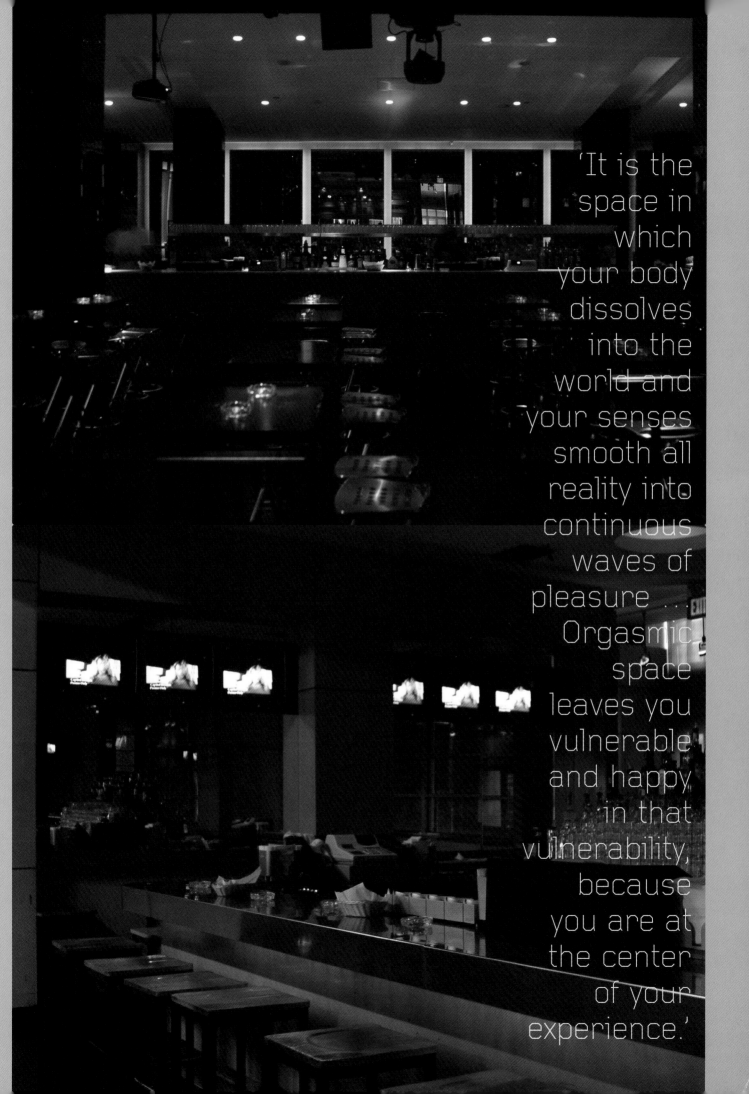

'It is the space in which your body dissolves into the world and your senses smooth all reality into continuous waves of pleasure ... Orgasmic space leaves you vulnerable and happy in that vulnerability, because you are at the center of your experience.'

evident. But Betsky notes that in so doing only the body and bodily pleasures remain. Within the sphere of contemporary Chelsea club-life, themes and variations on this defining principle are also evident. Yet while architectural analysis of Chelsea's gay club spaces responds, affirmatively or not, to the principle of orgasm, it is the physical experience of orgasm that is the platform for design.

An excellent example to communicate the terms of contemporary Chelsea orgasmic space is the David Barton Gym. The health club's steam room is the nucleus of gay sexual activity. If a visitor does not witness sexual acts taking place in the steam room, he can view their detritus: the room is littered with small plastic cups filled with moisturising lotion used as sexual lubricant.

Compared to the luxuriously appointed room or the farcical theatre, both of which are maximalist in their styling, the steam room accomplishes the goal of orgasmic space in an imperceptible manner. It is simply a tiled room with a built-in tiled bench running along its perimeter. Arguably, in a club that so clearly caters to a gay clientele, this is making an architectural point: anything more sensuous would possibly detract from the body, from the sexual programme in place. The steam, too, compels the occupant to focus solely on orgasm. It obscures the chamber's proportions as well as its occupants. It allows the user self-indulgent bodily pleasure – to be at the centre of his experiences – even if he is physically engaged with others.

As a place that permits gay men to achieve orgasm without forging bonds of identity, the steam room also provides other opportunities to explode social constructs. Just as architectural order disappears in the steam, so do the socially hierarchical qualities, such as age, that might preclude one man from having sex with another. In this sense it is a democratic place. It is also completely ironic: this exemplary polity is achieved only through a very private appropriation of the club's public space.

The gay man's appropriation of public space to achieve orgasm is not unlike the activity of cruising the city. Within the sphere of the very ordered city, the cruiser temporarily queers a space. And in this spirit of cruising, the David Barton Gym's exercise floor approximates the urban condition. It is an unremarkable space, with machines arranged in a grid pattern, exposed ductwork and the rubber-matted floor assuming the look of a dark-grey concrete.

Moreover, scope for cruising on the exercise floor is great, particularly because each object

of attention knows the meaning of the gaze and will potentially reciprocate. Almost every vertical surface, including the columns, is mirrored so that glances can be exchanged or bodies anonymously admired. The health club eschews ambient lighting in favour of downlighting, which accentuates individuals' musculature. And the arrangement of equipment creates certain bottlenecks – between rows, at nodes such as the water fountain or near the entry ramp – that amplify opportunities to interact with passers-by.

That designed, or preconceived, interaction is a priority resurfaces in a further interpretation of the floor plan of the David Barton Gym – the relegation of cardiovascular exercise to a separate area. In New York gyms such as Crunch, the cardiovascular machines are interspersed among the weightlifters, or ring the body-building equipment. At David Barton, however, cardio-exercisers have a semi-enclosed room of their own. Sight lines permit them, too, to ogle the muscle boys. Yet acknowledging that joggers and bikers have more in common with one another than with a man who can bench press hundreds of pounds, the gym's space offers a separate quieter, if smaller, space. Like begets like, in other words.

As a kind of processional that leads from the entrance through the hyper-urbanity of the exercise floor (or a tangent to the treadmills, if one wishes), and to the formless sexual fantasia of the steam room, the David Barton Gym is one of the most explicit examples of how clubs for gay, white men in the early 21st century New York handle the principles of queer space.

SBNY: A Near Equivalent

In establishing an alternative architecture that dissolves spatial as well as social orders, the David Barton steam room has its closest equivalent in another similarly architecturally formless landmark of gay orgasm. 'The Meat Rack' is the scrub forest immediately west of The Pines, a beach community on Fire Island east of New York City. The Pines is the place to which much of the New York gay social scene is transplanted during the summer, and not coincidentally the David Barton locker room includes material cues reminiscent of the seashore, for example travertine and coloured-glass floor tiles representing sand and beach.

Conversely, in many of Chelsea's gay club venues the steam room is a typology for design. Unlike the hierarchical breakdown that the steam room achieves, however, these derivatives of the steam room differentiate bodies. At sex clubs such as the West Side Club, club-goers invite others into cubicles that vary in size and price. The sex club borrows the steam room's bland box as a basic organising unit but in so doing reinstates social identity and hierarchy.

At nightclubs such as Splash Bar New York (SBNY), the steam room is desired but not achieved. One architectural

Opposite, top
The front bar at SBNY, seen from behind.

Opposite, middle
SBNY's third bar is located in the cellar. Note the black tile cladding the columns. The material can also be found in the bathroom of the David Barton Gym, and its reflective properties make it ideal for cruising.

Opposite, bottom
Overflow from the front bar can spill past or through the SBNY dance floor, towards the rear bar.

feature of the 12-year-old Chelsea club, which survived a recent renovation, is a raised platform in which the turn of a lever will activate a row of shower heads. It has become a stage for hired go-go boys. According to Warren Bohn, principal of Bohn Associates and architect of SBNY's renovation: 'We could have put a changing room behind the stage', however it was decided that the dancers should have to brush past the crowd instead. Once again, a hierarchy is established – of object versus subject, of visually superior go-go boy versus patron – that keeps the individual from achieving sexual release. The scene simulates all the activity of the locker room, minus the sexual release of the steam room.

SBNY imitates urban life as well. Although the club comprises 20,000 square feet, an intentional density greets the patron as he enters. Bohn

symbols. As operators of symbolic logic, we are increasingly post-middle-class, post-individual, post-body. There is no time or place for presentation, for family, for celebration, or for fear ... Queer spaces are disappearing, as are most spaces of experience.[2]

Chelsea's gay club spaces, from health club to sex club to bar, are not exclusive: membership is chosen not from an 'insider' elite, but rather is contingent upon self-selection and the ability to pay a regular fee or one-time cover charge.

Self-selection depends, of course, on one's personality and objectives. If looking for arousal, choose SBNY; for release, the West Side Club. If sex isn't the goal, an individual may choose another venue entirely. In the case of bars and nightclubs, whether or not a space affirms the tropes of the steam room serves as the architectural cue for making that choice.

'We are all becoming part of a consumer society in which there is a premium on interchangeable, malleable data, icons, and symbols. As operators of symbolic logic, we are increasingly post-middle-class, post-individual, post-body.'

explains that a bar is located immediately past the entrance so that patrons can enter at any time and see others present. Rather than escape from the city, SBNY stylises the urban experience. Overflow from this first bar moves back, past the shower stage, to another bar or to a bar in the cellar. Meanwhile, dark lighting, highly reflective surfaces in the form of black ceramic tiles, and a visible bathroom provide opportunities for the seduction of cruising.

Assimilative Design

At the same time, queers are disappearing. We are all becoming part of a consumer society in which there is a premium on interchangeable, malleable data, icons, and

In what may, then, be considered a split identity (between steam-room sexuality and visibility to the public), the renovation of SBNY involved installing floor-to-ceiling windows in the store front. This strategy originated at g, which opened in 1998. Here, a large glazed archway makes it clear to pedestrians that the space is being used as a gay bar. Queer space had come out of the closet.

The architect of g, James Bartholomew, had suggested the full-height windows to the client because 'there's nothing to be ashamed of – I wanted anybody to come here'. What is interpretable as a politicised gesture also moved the design to engage the urban condition in a completely different way: looking to the public at large, g demystifies the gay 'scene'. The walls are wrapped in birch plywood to create seemingly

Above right
The exterior of g is completely glazed to allow anyone to see inside.

Opposite
g opens to a lounge, with a bar behind it. Like the exterior, the interior comprises a series of symmetrical proscenium arches. However, the materials and seating give the interior a domestic appearance.

Below
The bar that greets patrons of
XL is two-sided for better
cruising, and is slightly bowed
in order to create a traffic
bottleneck between the lounge
and the stairway behind it.

Opposite, top left
XL is an escapist landscape
with fantastical ceiling lighting.
The lighting grid was designed
by Leni Schwendinger Light
Projects.

Opposite, top right
The crowd at XL.

Opposite, middle
XL's exterior of sandblasted
glass obscures the goings on
within, but neon lighting
announces it to the street.

Opposite, bottom left
XL's VIP room, located behind
the first-floor lounge, is walled
in one-way glass to permit
seeing out, but not in. It also
includes closed-circuit TVs so
that patrons can cruise the
bar; they can then phone the
host to invite guests to the VIP
room.

Opposite, bottom right
The bathroom median is
punctuated by a fish tank,
which diffuses sexual tension.

Notes
1 Aaron Betsky, *Queer Space:
Architecture and Same-Sex
Desire*, William Morrow and
Company, Inc (New York),
1997, p 17.
2 Ibid, p 14.

domestic warmth, and the open-plan room is the antithesis of the labyrinth of cubbyholes one might expect to find at a sex club, the pockets of darkness for which gay bars are notorious or the titillating diaphanousness of the steam room.

The g interior is not completely without SBNY's or the David Barton Gym's layers of seduction. Upon entering, a front lounge leads to a bar via slight segmentation of space. The bar itself is an oval, which Bartholomew explains allows a figure-8 circulation between the two vignettes, and was designed specifically with cruising in mind. The pattern repeats between the bar and the bathroom, which can be entered or exited on two sides.

But what g omits is orgasmic space of both the literal and metaphorical varieties, because its interior also embraces the public at large. The unisex group bathroom, for example, has two entryways, but one is labelled 'men', and the other, 'women'. This free-for-all space is another gesture that demystifies the gay club experience by welcoming outside heterosexual patrons, and is a witty commentary on queerness and sexual ambiguity – if not a complete embrace of sexual ambiguity because it nevertheless holds on to gender categories. Moreover, it is too public to be appropriated for sexual use. There is no equivalent of a back alley at g. It is a living room. 'In my mind,' Bartholomew says, 'g was almost like an anti-gay bar.'

'Anti-gay' is a trend that is quickly overtaking gay club-life in Chelsea. Says David Ashen about bar and lounge XL, which opened in 2000: 'My client wanted to make it like a straight bar, if with an edge.' In this spirit, XL also announces itself in

the streetscape. The glazed exterior is sandblasted to obscure the occupants and activity inside. Instead, a vertical neon stripe is suspended above and in front of the glazing to establish a presence on an otherwise dingy street. Style trumps transparency.

In remaining self-contained, XL reinstates some principles of urbanity and orgasm. The entrance vestibule, by cloaking the new arrival in sandblasted whiteness, becomes a catwalk that lends itself to the objectification of the body as well as seduction (akin to David Barton's exercise floor); the sandblasted-glass bathroom cubicle partitions reveal parts of the body when pressed against them, allowing the same kind of sexually exciting anonymity afforded by steam.

It is none too easy to accuse Ashen of overdesigning this space. This is an over-the-top minimalism, in which every plane seems to float in front of a veil of LED lighting, and is an affront to the tenets of Modernism; total construction cost for the 4,600-square-foot bar was approximately US$2 million. Analogously, flamboyant style obstructs the sexual programme.

For example, sight lines from the mezzanine-level lounge or via the closed-circuit cameras in the VIP lounge, are not so much cruising but voyeurism. If the point of cruising is to make a momentary connection in space, these visual patterns foster disjunction and alienation. The bathroom, meanwhile, includes two troughs, a row of sinks and one of urinals, which share a common plumbing core. On top of this median, a fish tank diffuses the possibility of seduction. Instead of using architecture to parody architecture itself, the fish tank exposes cruising with a knowing, humorous wink.

Even without g's political statement, Chelsea's lazily neo-Modernist gay clubs show an assimilative group of patrons demanding mainstream design. The result falls short of the definitions for queer space that Betsky lays out.

Once upon a time, says Warren Bohn, 'gay bars were non-designed – they had a straight, back bar kind of feel. It's changed. People expect a reflection of their status, economically and politically.' But as g and XL make clear, perhaps we're back to where we started. Straight clubs look like gay clubs look like straight clubs. And where the similarities aren't perfect, ironic witticisms fill the void. Ashen wonders: 'Are the lines starting to get blurred and it doesn't matter any more, or are we losing our identity?'

Demarginalisation seems to run counter to queer architecture. The potentiality of queer architecture, as the David Barton Gym epitomises it, is great. With or without orgasm itself, the idea of deformation – either in the breaking down of historic geometries, based on the exposure of architectural orders as artifices, or as a recreation of an urban condition inside – represents some of the most exciting trends in contemporary architecture. Now, queer space seems poised to simply adopt trends as they develop, rather than set them. Δ

'Gay bars were non-designed — they had a straight, back bar kind of feel. It's changed. People expect a reflection of their status, economically and politically.'

'Tie Me Kangaroo Down — sport'

Sports Clubs in Australia

Lindsay Johnston discovers the paradox at the heart of a sporting nation, which despite its proliferation of clubs of every type has a dearth of high-quality sports clubs. Here he looks at some of the exceptions.

Australia carries the reputation of being, per capita, the most sports-orientated nation in the world. This is when measured in terms of international success in sports such as cricket, rugby union, swimming and athletics, and it must be remembered that the population of Australia is a mere 19 million, mostly huddled around the edge of a vast island continent that has a landmass nearly as big as the US. This small population has to be compared with, for example, the UK at over 60 million and the US at about 275 million. It must also be borne in mind that the tourist brochure image of perpetual blue skies, golden beaches and beautiful tanned bodies refers to a country with huge climatic differences ranging from the temperate coastal conditions of New South Wales to steamy northern tropical conditions in Queensland and the Northern Territory, to cooler, greyer weather in the south, to searing hot arid desert throughout the expansive middle, and to snow-covered alpine conditions in the mountains.

An overview of the sports and social club culture in, for example, the greater Sydney region, reveals that excluding nightclubs there are about 1,600 clubs over a wide spectrum ranging from sports, cultural, social and political groups to various minority-interest groups such as the NSW Coaster Collectors Club, or possibly the most eccentric, the New South Wales Fancy Rat and Mouse Club!

Of these 1,600 clubs, about 25 per cent are described as 'social–general', which includes the very powerful and culturally very significant group of workers' clubs and returned services league clubs (RSLS), which are not specifically associated with any sports facilities, and leagues clubs (associated with rugby league, the predominant field sport in New South Wales), all of which are, in most cases, luxurious leisure palaces with extensive entertainment, cabaret, bar and restaurant facilities, and with ample provision of 'pokies' (poker and other gambling machines), which are a large source of income.

About 15 per cent of clubs are cultural, community, political, ethnic and other hobby clubs of various kinds, leaving the great majority of 60 per cent – nearly a thousand in the Sydney region – identified as diverse sports clubs. Surprisingly, the largest category of this group is represented by 175 bowling clubs (lawn bowls). This reflects the abundance of fine weather and signifies that this sport, in Australia, is embedded in every small community providing, as well as bowling greens and associated sports facilities, extensive social, bar and restaurant amenities

very much along the lines of the workers' and leagues clubs. The make-up of the remaining clubs also reflects the sporting preferences of Australian society, with 90 golf clubs, 75 soccer clubs, 60 tennis clubs, 50 rugby league clubs, 50 surf life saving clubs, 43 yacht clubs, 25 rugby union clubs, strangely only 13 cricket clubs and 6 swimming clubs. After that there are numerous clubs for every conceivable sport, including five – probably too few – callisthenics clubs for 'exercises to cultivate gracefulness and strength'. In the other states of Australia, the profile is probably similar but with significant cultural, climatic or even tribal differences. For example, in Victoria and South Australia, 'footy' is the Australian-rules game – a seriously important national pastime derivative from Irish Gaelic football – as distinct from 'footy' in New South Wales, which is rugby league.

This huge club culture significantly moves social intercourse away from traditional 'pubs' – which are still widespread throughout Australia and traditionally known as 'hotels', whereas 'hotels' (with modern accommodation) are conventionally known as 'motels' – and the focus of much entertainment and relaxation after the sporting event, or even before and during, is the club bar and ancillary facilities.

It is extraordinary, therefore, that a scroll through five years' worth of back issues of Australia's two leading architectural magazines – *Architecture Australia* and *Architectural Review Australia* – reveals few examples of significant or award-winning sports club buildings, other than the many significant structures for the Sydney Olympics. Though a huge programme of building, renovation and rebuilding is on-going in the workers' clubs and RSL sector, much of it architect-designed, little of it appears to find its way into the realms of significant architecture. One would think that there would be abundant spectacular examples of the iconic surf life saving clubs found at almost every beach along the extensive coastline, or yacht clubs, or tennis clubs, or golf clubs, but this is not the case. Perhaps it is the fine weather that determines that clubhouses are not a high priority. The lack of publicly funded programmes for sports club facilities often results in poor budgets, and voluntary labour to achieve the necessary results. There is a fine dividing line between communal sports facilities provided by local authorities and government, and what are identifiable 'clubs'. The significant award-winning examples of outstanding architecture in sports 'club' contexts are predominantly projects that are publicly funded or located in publicly funded universities.

The emergence of a 'club culture' in Australia, manifest in built form, appears to have resulted from the period of national affluence in the early 20th century. An example is the exotic Bathers' Pavilion at Sydney's fashionable Balmoral Beach, designed on a Moorish theme by Alfred Hale, an architect with

Mosman Council, to provide changing facilities for erstwhile bathers. The symmetrical and ordered plan and consequent elevations, which showed no hint of an impending modern movement, present an imposing face to the sea and all who may enter there. This eccentric building, having lain in disrepair for some years while controversy over its future raged between authorities and local residents, has now been restored by award-winning architect Alex Popov and has reopened as a stylish 'on the beach' restaurant with interiors by McConnel Rayner.[1]

One of the first significant modern movement club buildings to arrive in Australia was the splendid and highly innovative Manly Surf Pavilion, the competition for which was won by architect Eric Andrew in 1936, with speculation that the subsequently highly influential architect Sydney Ancher may have had some part in the design. The selection and commissioning of this building were reflective of optimism for the future, Modernism being the built manifestation of a new egalitarian society, albeit darkened by the impending world war. The completed building won the prestigious Sulman Award of the Institute of Architects in 1939 but sadly was demolished in 1980 due to irreparable concrete cancer.[2]

Much later, in 1983, the name of Sydney Ancher is associated with the Queenscliff Surf Pavilion, which was designed by the practice Ancher Morlock and Woolley. This building followed the demolition of another, older

> The symmetrical and ordered plan and consequent elevations, which showed no hint of an impending modern movement, present an imposing face to the sea and all who may enter there.

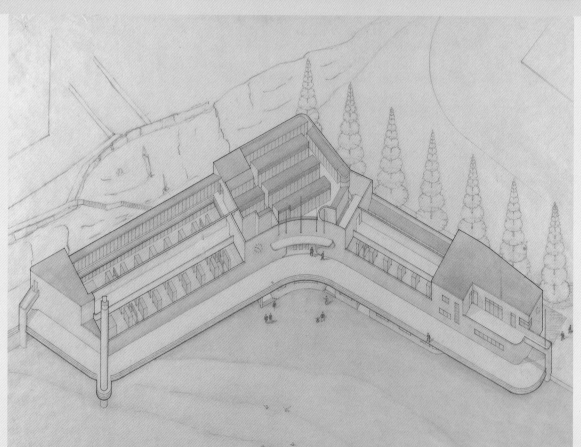

Above
Restored by Alex Popov in 1999, the Bathers' Pavilion at Balmoral Beach, Sydney, was originally designed by Alfred Hale in 1928.

Right
Original axonometric drawing by Eric Andrew, in the Mitchell Library, of the Manly Surf Pavilion, Manly Beach (now demolished), 1939.

pavilion that had deteriorated due to exposure to the lethal ingredients of sea, wind and sand. It continued the commitment by municipal authorities to invest in good local facilities designed by respected architectural practices. Very much of its time, the structure is directly 'on the beach' and, notwithstanding an interesting roof profile accommodated within a waveform roof metaphor, is distinctively Postmodern with clear nostalgic historicist references. In hindsight it could be seen to be a regression from the highly optimistic and progressive Manly design of 1936.[3]

Following from a period of strong European influence, especially from Aalto, in the 1960s, and in parallel with international Postmodernism's literal references to things past, throughout the 1980s a distinctive Australian architectural language was being consolidated that was responsive to climate and place. This built on the work during the 1970s of, for example, Glenn Murcutt and Richard Leplastrier, and celebrated truly Australian technology of corrugated steel, fibre cement flat sheet and structures, and detail with direct nautical references. Larger sports buildings of the period include Daryl Jackson's National Sports Centre Swimming Halls in Canberra

(1983) and Philip Cox Richardson Taylor's Sydney Football Stadium and National Tennis Centre, Melbourne (both 1988).[4]

As a subset of this identifiably Australian vocabulary, during the 1990s a strong local architectural personality developed in the Sunshine Coast region of Queensland, north of Brisbane, led by Gabriel Poole and including John Mainwaring and Lindsay and Kerry Clare. The Clares made their mark with innovative private houses and group housing that reflected a coastal vernacular with fine external detailing that explored climate-responsive lightweight buildings sympathetic to the subtropical environment with feather-edged eaves, layered sun-shading and battens, blurring of inside and outside spaces, and natural cross-ventilation.

The Clares' Ski 'n' Surf Pavilion at Bli Bli on the Maroochy River (1994) further developed their domestic work into a small public building. Commissioned by an enlightened local business client (and art collector), the pavilion was designed, documented and built in 16 weeks, replacing a previous building that had been lost in a fire, in order to be ready for that year's tourist season. Construction within this very tight time-frame required that the Clares be on site nearly all through the building process. It may also have precluded undue client interference in the design and allowed

Below
Ancher Mortlock and Woolley, Queenscliff Surf Pavilion, Sydney, 1983.

them to deliver an unfettered fresh, colourful and exciting waterside facility. The building is described as catering for 'a young "surfie" set ... and is enriched in its acknowledgement of water, sun, youth and sport'.[5]

Exploration of this exciting and dynamic southeast Queensland local architecture has been nourished by the establishment of the University of the Sunshine Coast campus at Sippy Downs. New buildings here pushed to new limits the application of screening and layering, steel framing and corrugated sheet, veranda typologies and novel ventilation strategies. They include the widely published University Library Building designed through a collaboration between John Mainwaring and Lawrence Nield and Partners (1997)[6] and the University Recreation Club (1997), designed by the Clares[7] (see case study).

The 1990s brought a huge building boom to Sydney due to the upcoming 2000 Olympic Games and spawned a plethora of sport-related buildings. Styled the 'green' games, the focus was, inevitably, the main stadium by Bligh Voller Nield in association with LOB Partnership.[8] Critics from more avant-garde Melbourne considered the architecture of the games to be a 'big yawn' – which probably failed to recognise the huge achievement in getting the projects completed. However, significant lesser buildings included the not insubstantial New South Wales Tennis Centre by Lawrence Nield and Partners in association with BDP (UK), the memorable archery building by Stutchbury and Pape, and, not least, the quirky public toilets by Durbach Block and Nicholas Murcutt.[9]

Back at the water's edge, Sydney saw a number of design competitions for a swimming pool at North Sydney, the famous Boy Charlton Pool at Lady Macquaries Point around the corner from the Opera House, and a pool at Ultimo, won respectively by Ken Maher of Hassell Architects (see case study), Ed Lippmann Associates and seminal Australian architect Harry Seidler. Another iconic swimming club at Sydney's famous Bondi Beach, known as the 'Icebergs' due to the year-round swimming activities it offers, has recently been rebuilt to a largely

Below
Lindsay and Kerry Clare, Bli Bli Surf 'n' Ski Pavilion, Sunshine Coast, 1994.

commercial brief, designed by Marchese + Partners with a fine restaurant by Howard Tanner Architects.

In Victoria, which prides itself architecturally in a more explorative approach than elsewhere in Australia and is home to some of the country's most experimental designers, there is surprisingly only a limited harvest of outstanding sports club buildings. Internationally published award-winner Gregory Burgess has completed a building at Woolamai Surf Club, and Melbourne's Design Inc has completed a similar small surf life saving club at Wye River, partially funded by the 'Lifesaving into the 21st Century' grants programme. The practice Six Degrees, more renowned for designing fashionable bars, has implemented a skilled master-planning exercise that has led to the rejuvenation of Kooyong Lawn Tennis Club, one of 'old' Melbourne's social and sporting establishments, known as 'the home of Australian Tennis' (see case study).

Conclusion

Australia's predominance in the world of sport may be matched by its investment in sporting facilities for major sports, such as football in its various guises, and for large events such as the Olympic Games, but there appears to be no abundance of remarkable sports club buildings that are architecturally expressive of the great sporting, nautical and beachside culture of the country. The best architecture is largely coming from public-funded projects, and the excitement, innovation and 'Australia-ness' demonstrated, for example, in the Clares' small privately funded Bli Bli Pavilion should be an inspiration to other private or member-owned sports clubs to manifest their culture and spirit – wellbeing, optimism and success – through the design of their buildings. Kooyong Lawn Tennis Club has repositioned itself with a younger clientele – the future – largely through the design quality of its new buildings. Other sports clubs need to similarly find the ways and means to fund their new buildings as a manifestation of their sporting ethos that will again capture the great optimism and architectural invention shown in Eric Andrew's Manly Surf Club way back in the 1930s.

Below
Marchese + Partners, Bondi Icebergs Club, Sydney, 2002.

43

Lindsay and Kerry Clare (now Architectus)
University of the Sunshine Coast Recreation Club
Sippy Downs, Queensland, 1997

The good architecture of southeast Queensland is distinctive and has a dialect that reflects the hot climate and proximity to the beach, being quite different from, for example, Victoria to the south. A very enlightened approach to the procurement of new buildings at this new university campus was no doubt influenced by the presence of leading local architect Lindsay Clare on the university council. Other highly regarded local architects and nationally established practices were brought together to produce an interesting campus master plan and a truly regional architecture that has been informed by the strengths, and even quirkiness, of a recognisable local modern vernacular. After several very successful buildings had been completed through his positive influence, Lindsay Clare and wife Kerry were rewarded with a commission to design a small sports club building on the new campus.[10]

Following from their Bli Bli Surf 'n' Ski Pavilion (1994), the Clares were again confronted with a speedy design and construction programme and completed the Sippy Downs recreational club building in only 16 weeks – 6 weeks for design and documentation and 10 weeks for construction. The building is simple and robust, and provides flexible accommodation for sport-related activities including a football club, gymnasium, meeting room, occasional classroom and dance hall. It was required to be expansible in the future and to allow separate and parallel use of the main hall, with bar and servery, and the changing room facilities. These elements are segregated in plan and separated by a through veranda.

The club's location and orientation was dictated by the established master plan for the campus, designed by Aldo Giurgola (architect for Parliament House in Canberra), and its relationship to the layout of the playing fields, which committed the building to a north–south axis. Thus the building plan and section diagrams are driven by resolving the difficult long facades presented to the low east and west sun – usually avoided in this subtropical climate – and the need to induce maximum cross-ventilation. The roofs are stretched out over large verandas to the east and west to provide shade and reduce glare, and a monitor rooflight down the centre of the section throws light into and, using natural stack effect, draws air out of the centre of the building. The structure has been designed to withstand cyclone loadings and shows developments from the Clares' residential buildings with plywood box beams and hardwood columns and trusses bringing the key elements to the centre, thus freeing up the external walls. The side walls are permeable with large door openings and extensive glass louvres, and the veranda floors are stepped down to form a viewing platform for sports on the fields.

Along with the nearby library building by John Mainwaring and Lawrence Nield, the architecture of these Sunshine Coast University buildings is well-refined critical regionalism. The recreation club sits naturally in the treeless horizontality of the landscape and responds appropriately to the intense climate, like a 'half glider, half jump jet, deftly layered with broad overhangs',[11] reminiscent of the bush classrooms of old that were no more than a roof over an open multi-use space below.

Below
Lindsay and Kerry Clare
(now Architectus), University
of the Sunshine Coast
Recreation Club, 1997.

44

Six Degrees
Kooyong Lawn Tennis Club
Melbourne, Victoria, 2000

The practice Six Degrees, as well as acquiring a reputation for refined interiors and bars, has been actively involved in rescuing buildings from extinction or desecration, notably the renewal of Melbourne's Capitol Theatre originally designed by Walter Burley Griffen and Marion Mahony (designers of Australia's capital Canberra), and other such projects as the adaptive reuse of a beautiful old convent in the spa town of Daylesford. The practice has also been undertaking master-planning consultancy for sporting facilities across the state. These attributes were recognised during a selection process, from a short list of six firms, as relevant to the task of bringing new direction and vitality to the so-called 'home of Australian tennis' at the reputedly 'Melbourne establishment' Kooyong Lawn Tennis Club. The firm's proposed master plan reconciled what was described as a 'planning nightmare', and its design profile was aligned with a more youthful market, which the club identified as crucial to its future.

The club, first contained in an Arts and Crafts bungalow by Cedric Ballantyne in 1923, has undergone a succession of alterations and additions by several other leading architectural practices, including a 1928 extension by a then young Edward Fielder Bilson, who had been Walter Burley Griffin's first articled student. This eclectic assortment of buildings thus presented a challenging imperative to unify the whole into a coherent and workable facility. Professor Philip Goad, in his *Monument* review,[12] suggests that Bilson's work gave Six Degrees cues that informed the practice's eventual strategy to highlight the original bungalow and reinstate original features including the porte-cochere and, even, suburban landscaping. Goad quotes 1927 *Home Beautiful* which eulogised that 'after a vigorous bout on the courts, the clubhouse must be home and mother and kindly nurse all in one'. The new refurbished clubhouse incorporates bars, dining rooms, function rooms, a gymnasium and indoor swimming pool.

Melbourne architecture is identifiably different from Queensland or Sydney styles and is, to the outside observer, less informed by climate and place and more informed by cultural references and abstract theory. This can, at worst, present as overly fashion-conscious, albeit provocative, realisation that will, like fashion, be ephemeral and quickly date. The work of Six Degrees is more substantial and, while reflecting the rich cultural traditions of Melbourne, delivers great dexterity of strategy and detail. The new-generation Kooyong is a transformation that carries off a marriage between the starchy traditions of a club for the city's upper crust with an architecture that is young, thoughtful and accomplished. The success of this architectural makeover is evident in the intensive use of, and extensive waiting list for, membership of this exclusive club.

Below
Six Degrees, Kooyong Lawn Tennis Club, Melbourne, 2000.

Notes
1 Davina Jackson, 'Bathers', *Architecture Australia*, Architecture Media Australia (Melbourne), vol.89, no 1, Jan/Feb, 2000, pp 44–9.
2 Andrew Metcalf, *Architecture in Transition – the Sulman Award 1932–1996*, Historic Houses Trust (Sydney), 1997, pp 70–1.
3 Jennifer Taylor, *Australian Architecture Since 1960*, Royal Australian Institute of Architects (Canberra), 1990, p 202.
4 Ibid, pp 235–7.
5 Peter Hyatt, *Local Heroes – Architects of Australia's Sunshine Coast*, Craftsman House (Sydney), 2000, pp 192–7.
6 Davina Jackson and Chris Johnson, *Australian Architecture Now*, Thames and Hudson (London), 2000, pp 168–73.
7 Ibid, p 83.
8 Lindsay Johnston, 'Green limits in a land of plenty', *Architectural Design – Green Architecture*, Wiley-Academy (London), 2001, pp 52–9.
9 Davina Jackson and Peter Hyatt, *The Games Show – Australia 2000*, Peter and Jennifer Hyatt (Melbourne), 2000.
10 John Hockings, 'Clubland', *Architecture Australia*, Architecture Media Australia (Melbourne), vol 87, no 1, Jan/Feb, 1998, pp 64–9.
11 Peter Hyatt, 'Learning curves', *Steel Profile*, BHP (Melbourne), no 64, June, 1998, pp 10–13.
12 Philip Goad, 'Detail game', *Monument*, Terraplanet (Sydney), no 20, Feb/March, 2001, pp 77–81.
13 Elizabeth Farrelly, 'Ribbons of light', *Architecture Australia*, Architecture Media Australia (Melbourne), vol 90, no 3, May/June, 2001, pp 44–9.

Right
Hassell Architects, North Sydney Swimming Pool, 2001.

Under the shadow of the iconic Sydney Harbour Bridge, and beside the equally iconic laughing face of Luna Park pleasure ground, the North Sydney Swimming Pool is located on a site to die for, overlooking the harbour and city skyline with the Opera House offstage left. The constituency of this club is exclusive in a different way. Open to anyone who is serious about swimming, it embraces the existing open-air pool built for the 1938 Empire Games and adds a new indoor 25-metre pool and supporting facilities. The original pool by Rudder and Grout has hosted numerous world records and is frequented by committed lap swimmers. The implemented design was the winning entry in a two-stage design competition that was well managed, largely without controversy, and gained the client, North Sydney Council, an award from the Royal Australian Institute of Architects for 'Innovation in Local Government'. One wonders if the commitment to this worthy procurement process may have been influenced by the fact that the wife of the mayor was an architect!

The brilliant design stroke of Ken Maher and team in their winning entry was to locate the new pool to the north of the existing pool, on a shelf above and overlooking the original pool, allowing full appreciation of the dramatic aspect and opening up a garden terrace, to the north again, that could capture sunlight (the sun is in the north in the southern hemisphere). Elizabeth Farrelly, in her *Architecture Australia* review,[13] quotes a comment from one of the judges: 'Shining simplicity and brilliance'. Though it went through various iterations, the design retained the essential features of the first sketches. Farrelly observes: 'Successively shimmering layers of horizontality – ceiling, water, water, water', the three waters referring, in descending order, to the new pool, the old pool and the harbour. The plan and section solve a multilevel entry itinerary and integrate the old pool and the new, with a spectator seating area, sun deck, restaurant, gymnasium, changing rooms and supporting services. The primary roof integrates the structure with the rooflight slots, and a system of roof-mounted solar collectors heat the pool and supply hot water.

In comparison to the Queensland and Victoria examples, this scheme is devoid of any appreciable 'dialect', but speaks quietly and deals locally and ingeniously with the complex geometries (and politics) of the place, cleverly working the medium of sun and natural light, opening up the boundaries between inside and out, and maximising the potential for ventilation and bringing the outside inside and the inside out. △

The High-Flying World of Clubs

Eleanor Curtis looks at the way British Airways has imbued the physical identity of its clubs' facilities with a sense of luxury and exclusivity, engendering a sense of privilege to its millions of members.

Above left
British Airways' Club Lounge at JFK Airport, New York
In contrast to the cool, neutral palette at London's Heathrow, the lounge at JFK makes use of bold bright colours in waves and lines, and has 1970s-style swivel leather chairs.

Above right
British Airways' First-Class Lounge at London Heathrow Airport, Terminal 4
A soft, comfortable palette of neutral colours and the use of wooden screens give an otherwise artificial environment a hint of the natural. Designs by Futurebrand.

The British Airways' 'Club' boasts four million members.[1] This is an impressive number for a club – as many people as the population of a major European city. Four million is a large figure to manage, let alone to pamper and make feel special. The number alone challenges our usual ideas of clubs being typically private and exclusive, even cosy and intimate, with club owners on first-name terms with their members. However, in the context of world travel, and compared with the even larger number of 44 million passengers BA carries each year from one place to another, perhaps it is not so out of place.

Clubs, Cards and Miles

BA's Executive Club is the overall term given to its frequent-flyer programme that encourages passenger loyalty by offering a sense of belonging (to a club) through the mile-counter. It is free and open to any customer who wishes to sign up to count his or her miles and enjoy privileges that are rewarded dependent on the amount of accumulated zeros.

Like many other new 'clubs', the key to entrance is a credit-card-sized colour-coded card, one swipe of which reveals a whole file of personal information related to the card holder. Just as accumulated miles can be exchanged for privileges and flights with BA, points accumulated with Sainsbury's Nectar card or Tesco's Clubcard can be exchanged for food items and other goods. This whole process of exchange via the identi-card encourages a sense of belonging to a club, even though neither BA nor the above-mentioned supermarkets have a club in the physical sense of a place for their members.

Closer scrutiny of BA reveals a world of 'clubs' (Concorde, First Class, Club World, Club Europe,

World Traveller, etc) where, quite simply, the higher up the class system you go, the better the facilities. This is a world of clubs that is colour-coded gold, silver and blue (cards); a world of divides (curtains and doors); a world of seats and beds and coloured cushions; a world of menus and magazines and miniature cutlery; a world of information at your fingertips. In essence, it is today's world of travel, with that little bit more.

Superclub, as it was first known, referred to BA's business class, but since 1988 has carried the name Club World. More recently, since 1996 the airline has upgraded its image to that of a 'classy carrier' for its so-called millions of 'members'. Club World is still the name given to its long-haul business class, but differs from Club Europe, which covers its European business-class flights. (In fact, flying across the Atlantic produces roughly one-third of BA's revenue and as much as 90 per cent of its profits.)[2] First Class is the airline's top tier, and it is both Club and First that enjoy the greatest variety of 'club benefits', for example preflight lounges and exclusive on-board cabins. Further down the long-haul aisle are the recently revamped World Traveller and World Traveller Plus, which though they offer upgraded facilities are at the same time available to the budget-conscious traveller.

Club World

BA's Club World is new and inviting. Incorporating the latest in design, technology and trends in soft furnishings, it is now in a league of its own. The term 'Club World' has been realigned with a whole batch of new product designs for all of its ground and on-board clubs, to the tune of £600 million, giving it a very strong identity indeed. To travel with Club World is to belong to BA's privileged class of travellers.

'Club World is a product descriptor of our long-haul business-class product to build a sense of belonging to a "club" of four million like-minded customers,' says Neal Stone, design manager of BA's in-house design

department. 'Membership in the traditional sense therefore starts with booking and ends with arrival. We wanted to build a sense of belonging for travellers with a similar need-state who were travelling the world on business. Club has since become the industry's generic term for business class.

'It originated from Superclub, which was one of the first separate cabins designed for business-class travellers and needs {in the 1960s}. This became Club World, which was launched in 1988. Its aim was "to deliver you ready for business".' And this is exactly what BA's world of clubs can do.

With the emphasis not only on high-tech gadgets and luxury creature comforts, BA's Club World and First-Class lounges and cabins have also led to the creation of some very sensible everyday design solutions, most notably the very practical use of the limited space in the cabins. And throughout the entire design–development cycle, the airline has always kept its focus on the customer, informed by extensive and continuous market research.

Club 69

When BA's design management team asked its frequent flyers what they wanted, the general wish-list included privacy, a good night's sleep,

flexibility, more space and more comfort. This wish-list was put out to tender to a variety of product-design companies. After internal and external reviews, Tangerine, a London-based company previously unknown to the airline industry, was selected, due to its fresh approach, to work on the new Club World. The brief was to create 'a lounge in the sky', a new concept that would allow BA to surpass its competitors and be unique, and would be flying within 18 months.

According to the airline customers' wishes, and to the industry's tight regulations (especially concerning weight), Tangerine was able to offer a radically new idea: 'First Class had already delivered the bed – introducing the horizontal concept – and our business-class passengers had aspirations based on what they had seen in First,' recalls Martin Darbyshire of Tangerine. 'The developmental constraints were also challenging. But as product designers we saw the seat as the main focus for the customer. The passenger can work on a seat but they also want to sleep. So we did some research into sleep.'

The Fidget Factor

After consulting with sleep experts, Tangerine established that to be able to sleep well we need to be able to move around, and to move around we have to be flat – 180 degrees flat. The company needed to design a seat-bed that would be comfortable enough to work on, eat from and watch TV from, and also sleep on with

Above
Tangerine's concept sketch of Club World's Club 69, whereby the seat-beds wrap around each other.

50

room to fidget so that customers could achieve the quality of sleep they required. The key to the design solution was a common-sense approach to the use of space: the company turned the 6-foot beds around into a '69' configuration and managed to get eight seat-beds in one row in the tight cabin space.

'We optimised the space for Club 69. We could give length to the bed without losing numbers. The physical configuration was a viable business plan for BA but also offered a much more casual environment. It really gave them the "lounge in the sky",' says Martin Darbyshire.

The 69 seats are arranged in forward- and rear-facing pairs with a fan-shaped screen in between to create private spaces, if desired, where passengers can eat, sleep, work or relax without being disturbed by other passengers. However, if customers wish to sit next to a companion, Club World also has conventional side-by-side seating. The passenger is able to control his or her environment to some extent – he or she can move around, be private, alter the seat angles when upright or sleep at 180 degrees when flat.

The seat-bed has gone on to win awards from both the design and travel industries, including the Grand Prix at the International Design Effectiveness Awards and the Marketing

Above left
Getting comfy: head to toe with fellow passengers in Club World's 69 chair configuration designed by Tangerine.

Above right
Club World on board. The 69 configuration of the seats allows more chairs per row than the traditional forward-facing seating.

Society's Award for Innovation.

In addition to the 6-foot flat-bed, Tangerine also gave Club World a swivelling footstool that stands at the end of the bed, is fully adjustable in height and can also be stowed away to allow easy access to and from the seat.

The response to Club World's Club 69 has been astonishing even in the relatively bad market of the last few years. Though the concept of backward-facing seating was initially seen as a negative, Club 69 has challenged this position in creating this successful design solution. BA has also patented the geometry and hardware of the design, restricting the design development of other airlines using their own 180-degree flat-beds.

Connect in the Air
In the field of high-flying telecommunications, Club World is also offering interactive broadband connections in the air. (The system, known as Connexion by Boeing, has been on trial since February this year.) Passengers can now use email and surf the Net while relaxing in their sky lounge.

Though broadband as a way of attracting passengers is being introduced by more than one airline, perhaps many passengers actually see their long flight as a welcome opportunity to escape from the world of information and real time. The use of the Internet in the air is still on trial, and as flying time is 'dead time' and time for passengers to switch off, not

on, perhaps it may not be such an attraction despite its technological sophistication.

Lounging in the Sky

The Club World 'lounge in the sky' cabin has been given its soft finishing touches by interior designer Futurebrand. In fact, the airline's entire product portfolio has been upgraded to include a whole range of brand signatures on anything from cushions to cutlery, tables and chairs. In addition to Futurebrand, which was brought on board for Club World's cabin interiors and lounges, BA's design team also commissioned Sir Terence Conran for its Concorde cabins and Concorde lounges at London Heathrow Terminal 4 and JFK, and Kelly Hoppen for its First-Class cabins.

The 'lounge in the sky' includes brighter seat fabrics, carpets, curtains and wall coverings, cashmere blankets in cranberry, blue and sage, 'crisp cotton pillows with Oxford borders', and black-and-white photographic prints on the cabin walls – all created to make the passenger feel more at home.

Lounging on the Ground

In keeping with the more traditional characteristics of clubs, BA has emphasised the lounge as a pre- and even postflight experience of membership.[3] As part of the £600 million refurbishment, a new concept has been given to the pre-lounge in the sky, that is to the real

'lounge on the ground' experience (at both London's Heathrow and New York's JFK airports).

The latest departure lounges available for Club World or First-Class members offer the new 'terraces' concept whereby they are compartmentalised into 'zones' dedicated to different activities. These include the Combiz Centre for communications and business needs, the World Wine Bar, Library, Larder, Cappuccino and Juice Bar, the Sanctuary and the Terrace Gallery.

For a relaxed garden/conservatory feel the Terrace Gallery uses garden furniture, indoor plants, pergolas and table umbrellas to create an unstuffy airport ambience. Oak flooring, rugs and garden sounds from a water feature enhance a peaceful setting, and natural light is maximised via large glazed windows and skylights. Such an atmosphere sits in stark contrast to the busy artificial world of retail, passage and information outside in the main airport.

The Sanctuary zone is a place for rest and relaxation, as its name suggests. Dimmed lighting, acoustic curved screens for privacy and discretion, day beds and recliners, and tranquil sound effects all contribute to the atmosphere of this laid-back lounge.

The First-Class lounge was opened at London's Heathrow in early 2001. In line with the on-board designs by Kelly Hoppen, BA brought in interior design company Futurebrand to create an 'elegant, calm and welcoming ... home-from-home space' (sic). Using rich velvets and the classical tailored herringbone to dress its chairs, tan leather for its recliners, and deep plum colours for its sofas, the First-Class lounge is an environment of exclusivity and class. Low, square

Above left
British Airways' First-Class Lounge at London Heathrow Airport, Terminal 4
Soft furnishings, neutral palettes and token *objets d'art* give the lounge its cosy club feel. Designs by Futurebrand.

Above right
British Airways First-Class on-board toilet
A fish-eye view into the BA First-Class toilet with mock-walnut panelling and black-and-white stills. Designs by Kelly Hoppen.

coffee tables front on to a wall of limestone and there is a hint of the colonial with its vertical arrangements of bamboo and exotic leaves, and linen-textured wallpaper. Again, screens are used as dividers, offering discrete areas in an otherwise public space. Art works by various known artists are platformed on walls or shelves, and curated by Artwise as part of the British Airways art collection.

If you enjoyed reading this article, then you might be interested in *Jetliner Cabins* by Jennifer Coutts Clay (ISBN 0470851651), available to AD's readers for an exclusive price of £24.99 (almost 30% off rrp). All you have to do is quote the code CQM when you order directly through John Wiley & Sons Ltd, and you will receive the book at the special price (+p&p). Offer ends 31st January 2004. Order using any of the methods listed at the back of this issue or by visiting www.wileyeurope.com ensuring that you quote the promotion code to take advantage of this offer.

CD Partnership, Sir Terence Conran's architecture and design collaboration, created the Concorde room, which also opened early in 2001. Boasting quality materials – etched glass, Jura limestone, satin stainless steel, granite and marble, leathers, linens and black walnut wood-panelling – the Concorde lounges could easily pass for the ultimate in preflight luxury. The furniture is a collection of 20th-century classic and contemporary designs. The 'smoking room' features Hoffmann Villa Gallia sofas in a luscious red velvet with black-and-white piping, Eileen Gray Bibendum chairs in black leather and Patrick Caulfield's themed art works Grey Pipe and Cigar.

Both lounges offer Internet access and telecommunications at the fully equipped business centre. However, exceeding all expectations of a top-class 21st-century travel experience is the Molton Brown Spa situated at London Heathrow's Terminal 4. Exclusive to BA's Concorde, First-Class and Club World passengers, or holders of Gold or Silver cards, according to the company's press release the Travel Spa offers 'a ground-breaking range of performance services from sleep enhancers to nerve stabilisers, to a mind sharpener' – the ultimate in luxury travel!

Hurtling Through the Skies

BA's world of clubs has created a very different experience in long-haul air travel. More typical travel experiences remain in the the vast dome of the airport, sealed off from the real world, with its artificially lit shopping malls and rows of immovable seating. It is a place of movement, information, queues and retail. Contrary to the stillness and calm of the club's lounges, there is nothing discreet about the airport environment.

Passengers are removed from the real world while in this state of transit; they are moved over vast spaces, from place to place (and quite often while remaining still). The rhythms of the normal world are replaced with the rhythms of the airport and the airlines' preset spaces on board. The travel itself – the airborne experience – is yet another world that also removes the passenger, this time from the vastness of the skies and the technological complexity of the planes. Passengers are delivered to a place of designated spaces, orderly lines and queues, comfort and familiarity. Club World and BA's world of clubs have perfected this desired removal from the abstraction and discomfort of flying to the luxury of a 'lounge in the sky'.

BA's designs for its clubs have really taken the concept of travel comfort in the air and on the ground to the max. However, has this emphasis on design emptied the real experience of travel and flying and instead made it something completely empty of the reality of travel, albeit very comfortable. Seated on a plane, (or lying flat if in Club World), 33,000 feet above the ground, we are literally hurtling through the skies. TV screens in the seats in front keep on providing us with bits of information related to how cold it is outside, how high we are, how fast we are going and when we are going to get there.

Today's design of the cabin and all that is offered to us in the cabin moves away from this idea. Is this because it is something too abstract or even too frightening to deal with? The most advanced Club cabins now offer the use of the telephone and access to the Internet in-flight. Will they also offer us flight-simulator games and other such techno toys that touch on the real thing?

Even Neal Stone of BA's design team admits: 'I'm not sure that aeroplane cabins are places that people would choose to be. But I'd like to think that Club World is such a good experience that customers enjoy spending time with us.'

BA's clubs are not really clubs in the sense of providing a social experience with other like-minded people. Rather, they try very hard to emulate the feeling of belonging to a club by dishing out privileges and special treatment for the select few. Perhaps some travellers actually enjoy being head to toe with another traveller in Club 69, or perhaps BA's Club World more simply offers a way out from the mundane hassle of everyday travel. ∆

Notes
1 This number represents the four million members of British Airways' Executive Club, the generic title given to BA passengers who belong to the airline's frequent-flyer programme and enjoy a variety of privileges dependent on class of travel.
2 'Preparing for war: How British Airways boss Rod Eddington plans to survive the war in Iraq', *The Economist*, 15 February 2003.
3 BA has recently offered the new arrivals lounge at London Heathrow, Gatwick and South Africa's Johannesburg airports as places to refresh in after long-haul flights.

Traditionally the ocean liner or cruise ship has pilfered much of its design vocabulary from classic gentleman's clubs.

The Floating Utopia

Jonathan Bell explains how this architecture of physical as well as social segregation is making a comeback on the high seas, with the building of luxury cruise ships and tax havens.

Architecture is the physical imposition of systems of control on the chaos of open space. Physical interventions can separate, segregate, exclude and divide, through barriers of varying degrees of subtlety. This, arguably, is how architecture has always functioned; as shelter and protection, structured by degrees of scale and effectiveness. The Modernist programme focused on the creation of an egalitarian society, democratising the built environment through standardisation, repetition and the removal of these traditional hierarchies of form and decoration. For many, however, there remains a strong desire to preserve society's physical segregation, for reasons of security or political ideology.

In recent times these desires have manifested themselves, amongst other things, in the 'gated communities' of private homes, self-contained zones that provide their own civic code, amenity services and security. In the US, several gated communities are now seeking complete autonomy from federal control and the official tax regime (why, they argue, should residents in effect pay two sets of taxes – one to fund facilities on a state level and one for the local level?).

The architecture of segregation is by its very nature insular and self-serving, concerned only with its immediate environment. One of the most celebrated – and romanticised – examples of division through physical design is the ocean liner, a mirror of society's top-down structure, with lower decks equating to lower classes. This image has endured, and with it the very anti-democratic notion of the ocean liner as a somehow elitist space, the preserve of the wealthy.

Regardless of the reality of this situation (cruise-liner-based holidays, in particular, have become enormously popular in recent years), this essay is an examination of the role of social structure in floating environments, examining how elements of the perfect – even utopian – environment continue to be projected through ocean-going design. It also explores even more complex interpretations of the exclusive environment, 'floating utopias' that make a virtue of exclusivity using architectural design as an expression of a private, secluded place.

Perfecting these private places is an ongoing concern, whether in the design of hotels, private members' clubs, apartments or country clubs. Architectural considerations are everything – spaces of exclusivity need hierarchical levels of circulation, separating servicing from the serviced, the private from the public. A historic equivalent would be the traditional country house, with below-stairs and eaves accommodation, and hidden access arranged to serve the important rooms of the house while remaining discreetly out of view.

To the outsider, the existence of numerous lounges, clubs and staterooms on the world's grandest liners (some accessible only to first-class passengers), imitates the spatial and architectural separation found within land-based clubs. Arguably, one shouldn't consider a cruise ship a 'club' in the traditional sense; exclusive, yes, but a space that cannot dictate a membership. Passage on these ships is available to anyone who can afford it, making them no more a club than an expensive restaurant, a polo game or an upmarket boutique. Despite this, the ambience of a cruise liner is intended to convey exclusivity and belonging, and design elements and layouts, not to mention underlying social structures, mimic club design.

There are parallels to be drawn between ocean-going exclusivity and the carefully designed space of the private club – the way the silent, hidden world of an ocean-liner crew facilitates the ease of life on the upper decks, with privations increasing as one descends down through the classes. Paradoxically, the ocean liner was once a critical point of reference for the early Modernists, a vast megastructure (before that term entered architectural use) with highly efficient use of space. Le Corbusier in particular admired the great liners, adapting their monumental aesthetic for his iconic Unités in Marseilles and Berlin, even extending the visual metaphor to the sculptural gymnasium and play area on their roofs, mimicking the liner's great funnels. Corbusier noted that a liner offered luxury in minimal space, and posited that similar living conditions were feasible within the densely populated city. Corb's in/famous 'machine for living' was as much influenced by ocean-going technology as it was by cars, appliances and building systems – if not more so.

While the Unité was essentially democratic in its structure and layout, the classic-era ocean liner could hardly make a similar claim. Although populist travel on the great liners was widespread, with steerage class offering an extremely uncomfortable yet highly sought-after passage to a new life, the great floating palaces of the first half of the 20th century presented extreme design unity, albeit reserved only for the upper classes. But the liner was only a temporary retreat; its role as a mode of transport for both rich and poor negated its exclusive status, despite the highly segregated arrangement of the interior. Once air travel had destroyed the liner's primary market, the emphasis switched to cruising for leisure. Contemporary cruise liners have elements of social segregation – for example, different standards of accommodation – but ultimately are far more democratic spaces than their predecessors, with no commercial need for cramped steerage class, for instance.

Previous spread left page
The World pool deck.

Previous spread right page
Vignette drawing of
ResidenSea's The World.

Opposite, top
At ResidenSea's Fosen
shipyard, Norway, 15
September 2001.

Opposite, bottom
Profile of The World decks.

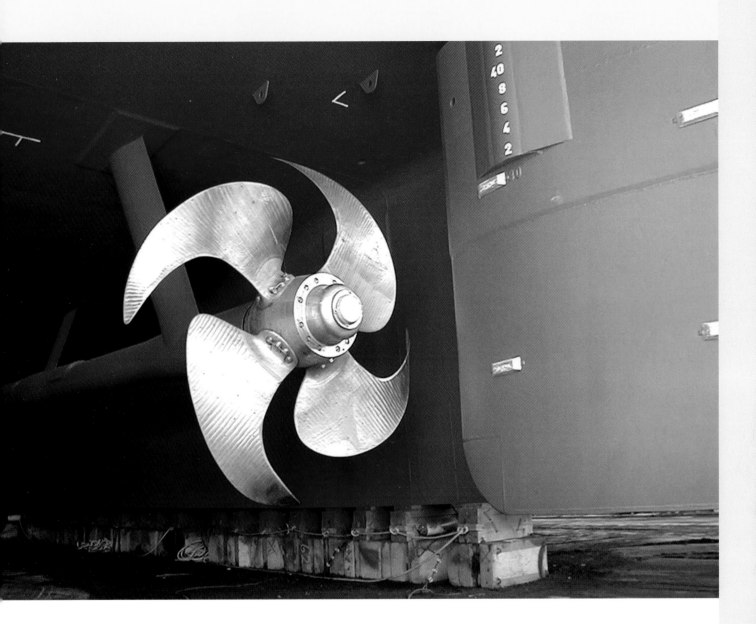

Decks
12
11
10
9
8
7
6
5
4

Le Corbusier in particular admired the liners, adapting their monumental aesthetic for his iconic Unités in Marseilles and Berlin, even extending the visual metaphor to the sculptural gymnasium and play area on their roofs, mimicking the liner's great funnels.

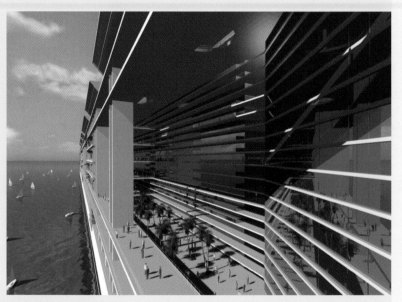

Above
The most recent designs for
the Freedom Ship.

Cruising is now accessible escapism, demand is rising and ships are swelling in size to accommodate this new popularity. Built in vast shipyards like Kvaerner's Masa-Yard in Finland (which accounts for 25 per cent of global cruise-liner production), or the Chantiers de L'Atlantique in Saint-Nazaire, the new breed of populist liners are characterised by their vast scale – frequently over 100,000 tons. Ocean-going behemoths such as Princess Cruises's *Golden Princess* and *Star Princess* (and the forthcoming *Diamond Princess*, *Sapphire Princess* and *Crown Princess*) have a gross tonnage ranging from 110,000 to 130,000, each catering for up to 2,600 passengers. The design is orientated around external views for the passengers, with balconies for the most upscale cabins, as well as towering internal atria complete with waterfalls, golf courses and casinos. Caribbean ports are dwarfed by the superstructure of these enormous beasts, their white flanks terminating century-old waterfront vistas like freshly constructed multistorey buildings. They are so large that passengers have to endure long queues to enter and exit their ships when they arrive in port.

The modern liner is a floating theme park, equipped with multiple entertainment areas and stages, discos and themed bars, presented as entertainment architecture, spaces that use drama, exaggeration and theatricality. They offer a plethora of family activities, representing the kind of democratic luxury and service that has come to be associated with multinational entertainment companies. Disney, for example, runs its own cruise line, sailing from Port Canaveral and taking in Caribbean or Bahamian destinations, with themed cruises such as 'Vow Renewal' or 'Family Reunion'. Interiors have more in common with the architectural exuberance of Maurice Lapidus or Jon Jerde, or the great atrium hotels of John Portman.

This is a curious inversion. As we have seen, the liner was once the muse of the machine age (and indeed survived as an iconic presence into the megastructural phase of the 1960s – see Hans Hollein's aircraft-carrier project of 1964)[1] – yet by the 1980s and 1990s nautical architects were apparently drawing their inspiration from land-based 'event' architecture. The heroic machine age is over. This is not to say that heroic machines are not still being built. Cunard's new $780-million flagship, the forthcoming *Queen Mary 2*, interior-designed by Tillberg Design of Sweden, is due to enter service in early 2004. The rear of the ship is given over to duplex staterooms and penthouses which can, if desired, be combined to create the largest 'cabin' in the world. It is estimated that a global cruise in this combined suite would cost around $4.25 million.[2]

Mass-market cruising is largely pitched at young families or time-rich retirees. But at the very top end of the market, where holidays stretch into months and can cost up to six figures, the concept of a permanent floating residence holds a huge allure for the world's ultrawealthy. Conceived by the Norwegian company ResidenSea, *The World* is a relatively modest liner at 644 feet long and 43,424 tons. Described as a 'mixed-use resort community at sea', the ship contains both traditional cabins and privately owned apartments. A three-bedroom apartment starts at around $4,342,000 for a 50-year lease, and can go as high as $7.5 million for 232 square metres of space, not to mention an annual service charge of 6 per cent of the purchase price. Just 390 paying occupants will have 'permanent' homes on the ship (perhaps because of its scarce, reclusive clientele, *The World* was initially derided as a 'ghost ship', with 25 per cent of the apartments still unsold six months after its launch).

The World set sail in March 2002, beginning a continuous global voyage from one exotic and glamorous location to another. This life in motion offers more than mere sightseeing: there are also substantial financial advantages. In the UK, nonresident status is awarded to those who spend less than 183 days a year in the country, meaning that *The World*'s British occupants escape paying income tax (it was suggested that all potential residents be income-tested, with a requirement of a minimum financial wealth of at least $5 million).

Cruising is now accessible escapism, demand is rising and ships are swelling in size to accommodate this new popularity. The new breed of populist liners are characterised by their vast scale. Ocean-going behemoths such as Princess Cruises's *Golden Princess* and *Star Princess* ... each cater for up to 2,600 passengers. The design is orientated around external views for the passengers, with balconies for the most upscale cabins, as well as towering internal atria complete with waterfalls, golf courses and casinos.

Below and following spread
Cunard's new flagship, the
forthcoming *Queen Mary 2*,
interior-designed by Tillberg
Design of Sweden, is due to
enter service in 2004.

Means-testing aside, what kind of environment could a potential resident of *The World* expect? In common with almost all cruise liners, explicitly contemporary interiors are the exception, perhaps because they fall foul of passengers' preconceived ideas of what exactly a luxury exclusive liner might look like. In comparison, the land-bound hotel industry (in particular the phenomena known as boutique hotels) thrives on architectural innovation and drama, and avant-garde designers frequently find themselves commissioned or quoted in the context of hotel design (for example the GrandHotelSalone at last year's Milan Furniture Fair, showed a concept hotel with room sets by the likes of Zaha Hadid, Ron Arad, Jean Nouvel and Arata Isozaki).

So why do cruise liners continue to eschew architectural innovation? Perhaps one should not underestimate the huge influence of cinema and television on our image of the liner – from *The Poseidon Adventure* to *Titanic* (the sense of impending yet romantic doom notwithstanding), Hollywood has compounded the reality of the great boats into a mass-market image consumed by hundreds of millions. *The World*, perhaps sensing that real exclusivity comes only through creating deliberate distance from the mass market, instead offers a selection of interior designers to complete your cabin (though purchasers of the smaller studio cabins get no choice; all work is carried out by the firm of Hirsh Bedner & Associates). More spacious residences can be designed by the likes of Nina Campbell (for 'timeless elegance'), Juan Pablo Molyneux (the 'sophisticated Continental home') and Sweden-based architects Yran and Storbraaten, who specialise in combining the 'nautical with the contemporary'.

The World is a club, but given that the exclusivity is closer to self-imposed isolation and the 'public' environments are beyond the residents' control, the emphasis has been placed on the interior world of the cabin. The four designers cited in *The World*'s publicity material (and you wonder just who is the most popular) are best known for their 'classic style', a Modernism that is neither revolutionary nor antagonistic, evoking wealth and ease, not physical dynamism or minimalist asceticism.

This is not to say that the contemporary cruise liner and its evolutionary relation, the private boat, do not emulate the aesthetic and social ideals of a private members' club. The signifiers of exclusivity and secrecy – maybe best illustrated by the wood-panelled members-only smoking room, occupied only by gentlemen of a certain class and forbidden to the majority of the population – are used to denote an indulgent, exclusive experience, regardless of the realities: that a cruise might be full of senior citizens, or young families, or reclusive millionaires unwilling to socialise. The architectural space of the liner has been distilled from the physical realities of the prewar luxury liners with their Deco twists, gilt touches and relentless emphasis on surface, materials and, it must be said, artifice.

Liners present carefully controlled interior worlds in opposition to public space: the closest parallel that can be drawn between *The World* and land-based architecture is the gated communities that have mushroomed in popularity in the last quarter century (one in six Americans live with some kind of separation from the 'public realm'). A floating gated community goes one step further, with none of the uncertainty that comes from 24-hour security guards, restricted access and extensive covenants and zoning guidelines governing activities.

Entrance to *The World* is already bound by a comparable series of strictures. All potential buyers have to complete a consent form that allows ResidenSea to run a 'detailed background check', which extends to credit rating (a net worth of $5 million is required) and criminal records, as well as verification that the 'buyer's worth has come from legitimate means'. There is also a 'personality check' and a meeting between ResidenSea and potential buyers. Like any upscale apartment building, the ship has a residents' committee, an elected group of seven that makes decisions on behalf of the 'on-board community'.

The World may one day be joined by even larger craft. Plans for a so-called 'Freedom Ship' have been circulating for a decade, gaining currency through an erratic website[3] and occasional, cynical articles in popular science titles and the lifestyle press. What sets the Freedom Ship aside from *The World* is scale: the proposal was for a $6.8-billion, kilometre-long vessel, a megastructural concept that moulded utopianism with elitism. Now that the proposal has apparently vanished in a haze of uncertainty, leaving puzzled fans to haunt the bulletin boards speculating on the scheme, it is easy to see how the Freedom Ship was far from Utopian. How, for example, could 30,000 residents and 10,000 crew interact in a vessel that must remain permanently at sea, physically too big to dock? How would the residents pass their time? Would it be little more than a vast empty floating mall, with no space for frustrated purchasers to use, store and parade their wares?

There have been other similar schemes. The Nexus Floating City, an eccentric 1986 proposal from California-based Tsui Design and Research,[4] described itself as a cooperative community where 50,000 residents would provide a payment (or a loan) of

between $100,000 and $200,000 to enter the 22-square-kilometre 'vessel' – in effect a self-sufficient island growing its own food and providing power from photovoltaic arrays and wind turbines. The population, broken down into several communities, would 'evolve' its own 'laws and principles'. There is also the Venus Project,[5] 'the redesign of a culture', a series of proposals for sea-based structures containing a sustainable, resource-based economy and eschewing conventional society, with its accompanying 'unemployment, violent crime, replacement of humans by technology, over-population and a decline in the Earth's eco-systems'.

The dominant theme is one of escape from the restrictions of conventional society, chiefly represented by a disdain for governmental intrusion of any kind. In the Caribbean, southwest of Cuba, visionaries are planning New Utopia,[6] an 'island paradise' with a political system derived from that of Monaco and pre-hand-over Hong Kong. The 'Principality of New Utopia' is described as an ideal society that will provide 'proof of the benefits of free market laissez-faire capitalism, without the mediation of politics'.

The Atlantis-styled project makes explicit reference to Ayn Rand's New Utopian theories as well as to the visions of the late science-fiction author Robert Heinlein, whose work included a strong libertarian streak – the philosophy of living according to one's own wishes and desires providing other people's rights are respected. Rand's novel *Atlas Shrugged*[7] depicted a society in the throes of destroying its 'prime movers', the achievers who dominated it socially and economically. To avoid destruction, these prime movers created a secretive new society, Galt's Gulch, seen by many as the forerunner of the libertarian ideal. New Utopia's wholesale avocation of Rand's purist form of capitalism – free from such encumbrances as welfare and taxation – is the driving force behind the project. Currently, New Utopia exists as little more than a website, and a similar venture, the unfortunately Orwellian-sounding Oceania,[8] rose on a wave of media interest in 1993, only to sink back beneath waves of apathy.

Are there any parallels between the exclusive yet ultimately nonpolitical space of the luxury liner, a space devoted to hedonism and display, and the politically motivated floating utopia concept? For now, *The World* acts as a bridge between the two spheres. The new generation of super-liners might provide a world of hedonistic self-interest, utterly unlike the packaged and predictable world of international tourism, but the floating utopia remains a pipe dream. These self-contained societies hinge on the ability of their residents to pay their way: individual civic contribution to these vastly expensive schemes can only be

measured monetarily. Crucially, these futuristic megastructures and private islands co-opt the aesthetic and ambition of visionary Modernism yet utterly reject the social intent at the heart of the Modernist programme.

Back in 1971, the 'Sea City' concept was exhibited, commissioned by Pilkington, the glass manufacturer, in association with Ove Arup and Geoffrey Jellicoe (who had previously produced a motorised city, Motopia, for Pilkington's promotional purposes in 1961). Sea City was sited on Dogger Bank and was a community for 30,000 people, young and old, with on-site jobs and facilities. The scheme represented one of the dying gasps of Modernism's utopian strand, with its socially and economically inclusive structure (only the patriarchal language of the day gives it away:

Notes
1 See Reyner Banham, *Megastructure: Urban Futures of the Recent Past*, Thames and Hudson (London), 1976, p 21.
2 Prices quoted from New Zealand Maritime's QM2 site: www.nzmaritime.co.nz/qm2/
3 www.freedomship.com
4 See www.tdrinc.com/nexus.html
5 See www.thevenusproject.com
6 See www.new-utopia.com
7 Ayn Rand, *Atlas Shrugged*, Random House (New York), 1957.
8 See http://oceania.org/
9 *TV21 Annual 1971*, Century 21, (UK); see www.tonystrading.co.uk/galleries/annuals/tv21.htm
10 Thomas More, *Utopia*, Penguin Books (Middlesex), 1965.

'Gleaming shopping arcades span the south side of the city, all under cover so that Mum doesn't get wet when she's staggering home with the week's provisions on a rainy day.')[9]

The floating utopia is the ultimate members' club, a Galt's Gulch of epic proportions. Paradoxically, while a conventional club offers a temporary respite from reality, these schemes are a full-time existence, a total separation from reality, the point where 'club' design is eschewed for libertarian, even survivalist, instincts. Identity, the key concept for conventional club design – whereby members can identify with their club and fellow members, either through overt branding and symbols or perhaps through a more subtle set of behaviour and response – doesn't apply. In a self-contained autonomous environment, one's very presence signifies membership – there's no need to impose identity through other means. Ironically, it seems inevitable that even the purest and most deserving utopian community would fragment into smaller social groups as clubs within clubs emerge. There's no better illustration of this than *The World*'s Golf and Country Club, the first such venture on a privately owned ship.

Through various forms of media, from blockbuster films to thriller novels, the cruise ship has evolved its own psychological landscape, a backdrop to drama and intrigue, a stage setting that is the perfect environment for escapism. It is safe to assume that regardless of the day-to-day realities of a cruise, this psychic geography somehow imprints itself on the passenger, imbuing the experience with a sense of the extraordinary, the romantic. Conversely, the all-encompassing environment of a residential ship such as *The World* rejects the availability of social interaction in favour of a more internal, withdrawn experience. Arguably, the residents aren't at sea to socialise; they're there to escape from the strictures of government and taxation. The floating utopias go even further, banishing all memory of conventional society.

Thomas More's satirical *Utopia* (1516) not only brought the word into usage but pioneered the creation of an ideal 'other' system as a means of providing a critique of reality.[10] The floating utopia concepts can be read as a similar critique yet, where More's ideal was centred around the individual's need to contribute to the common good, the contemporary version takes the diametrically opposite view, with the shared goal of self-interest as the primary unifying force in line with the dominant political philosophy of the proponents. Instead, the floating utopia's co-option of Modernist design principles – scale, planning, technology, not to mention the physical intensity of the megastructural concept – is channelled into creating an isolationist, indulgent society, the very opposite of the inclusive spirit of Modernity. ∆

The Eng...
the Lond...

shness of
n Club

Jeremy Melvin traces the cultural identity of contemporary London media clubs such as Groucho's and Electric House back to a first generation of 18th-century aristocratic gambling haunts and a second wave of 19th-century members' clubs with their grand bespoke architecture.

• • •

'We're pretty broad-minded here,' says a character about the Drones Club in PG Wodehouse's story 'Uncle Fred Flits By', 'and if you stop short of smashing the piano, there isn't much that you can do at the Drones that will cause the raised eyebrow and the sharp intake of breath.'[1] Peopled by feckless and leisured, but not all monied, members of the aristocracy, the Drones is at the centre of Wodehouse's universe. We learn quite a lot about it. Luncheon is frequently enlivened by the throwing of bread rolls, and less frequently showerings of sugar. As young men pass through its two smoking rooms, the causes of their miens, whether anxious, triumphant or harried, become the starting point for stories.

Those members lured into matrimony mark their impending change of status with a valedictory dinner, whose consequences structure many subsequent tales. Tuppy Glossop once bet Bertie Wooster that he couldn't swing along the rings above the club's subterranean swimming pool from one end to the other in full evening wear – having first taken the precaution of looping the last ring out of reach, causing Bertie to plunge, fully clad, into the water. In short it is a typical London club, where the architecture is an incidental prop to social behaviour or particular events that define a tightly knit community.

Clubs would not be clubs if they did not have an identity, or at least a purpose, before they indulge in architecture. The difference lies in the way architecture might make the purpose explicit, or conceal it. The first generation of London clubs, the aristocratic gambling haunts of St James's Street like White's, Boodle's and Brooks', were barely distinguishable in their designs from the town houses of their richer members. But when the *ancien régime* began to crack in the early 19th century, new clubs with new purposes began to emerge.

In these, as Pevsner put it in *The Englishness of English Art*, architecture is inclined to tell a story. He thought the way Charles Barry's Reform Club evoked the grandeur of the Renaissance Farnese palace was 'not strictly aesthetic',[2] and he might have applied the same argument to the pseudo-Grecian air of Decimus Burton's design for the Athenaeum, a couple of doors away on Waterloo Place. Unlike the earlier St James's clubs, these two and the Travellers between them use architecture to project an image, but it is an image of the purpose of the clubs that architecture dresses, and if we can understand the early 19th-century association of Greece with learning, we might now find the putative link between the Palazzo Farnese and democracy a little harder to swallow.

Club design gives a particular insight into the way architecture can affect an institution's identity. Gambling was so much a part of the lives of the members of the older clubs that it required little differentiation in architecture. They knew what they were going to do, and where they were going to do it. But activities like learning, travelling and political reform were less a part of common experience; their clubs demanded a distinct

Previous spread
The Gaming House, the sixth
in William Hogarth's sequence
The Rake's Progress,
supposedly set in White's,
conveys something of the
atmosphere of an 18th-century
gambling club.

Opposite
The atrium of Charles Barry's
Reform Club, 1837–40, which
evokes the grandeur of a
Renaissance palace, planned
around a central courtyard
rather than the Georgian town-
houses that accommodated
earlier clubs.

Above
The trick at the Zanzibar, as its
lead designer Julyan Wickham
remembers, was to engender
conviviality, therefore the bar
was shaped to encourage the
mingling of individuals and
groups. Mirrors made a small
space seem much larger.

Right
The floor level at Zanzibar was
slightly stepped so that the
eye level of those seated in the
dining booths was the same
as that of those standing at
the bar.

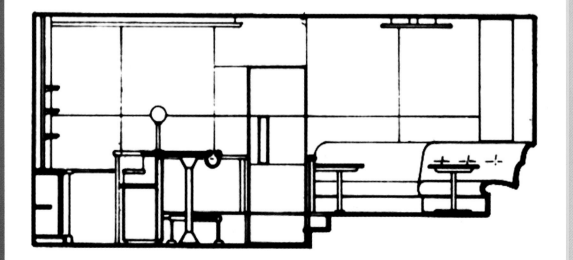

Opposite
At Groucho's, a rather larger
club than the Zanzibar, the
bar is the linchpin between the
entrance and the more
intimate dining areas.

Above
Tchaik Chassay's design for
Groucho's created an
atmosphere that incorporated
the eccentricities of the
existing building, including the
staircase.

Notes
1 P G Wodehouse, 'Uncle Fred
Flits By', in Young Men in Spats,
Herbert Jenkins (London), 1936,
republished by Penguin
(Harmondsworth), 1971,
pp 141–60.
2 Sir Nicholas Pevsner, The
Englishness of English Art, The
Architectural Press (London),
1956, republished by Peregrine
Books (Harmondsworth), 1964.
In Chapter 2, 'Hogarth and
Observed Life', pp 26–55,
Pevsner discusses what he
sees as a pervasive trend for
art in England 'to tell a story,
that is to put on a costume
chosen to conjure up certain
literary, evocative or
associational ideas' (caption to
image of the Reform Club,
p 51). On p 48 he suggests that
'in England there existed ... a
disposition in favour of
narrative ... [whose] effect is
evocative, not strictly aesthetic'.
3 Giuseppe Tomasi di
Lampedusa, Il Gattopardo,
Feltrinelli Editore (Milan),
1958, trans Archibald
Colquhoun, The Leopard,
Williams Collins Sons and Co
Ltd (London), 1961.
Republished as The Leopard,
with Two Stories and a
Memory, Collins Harvill
(London), 1988. Throughout
the novel the Leopard of the
title, Don Fabrizio, Prince of
Salina (loosely based on

identity. And if learning could be adequately
expressed in a Greek idiom, and travel through
a building that drew inspiration from foreign
architecture, reform was a harder nut to crack,
but crack it Barry did. Making use of a gas supply
– Pall Mall was the first of London's streets to
have such a utility – he installed great burners on
the outside of the Reform Club at a time when
street lighting was almost unknown. Inside, this
allowed the great chef Alexis Soyer – who later
improved the rations of troops fighting in the
Crimean War – to operate a far more
sophisticated kitchen than anywhere else in
London. Members might have been unsure as
to the direction and extent of political reform,
but at least their appetites were sated.

The abstractions and subtleties of political
reform are notoriously difficult to express in
architecture, and Barry tried several different
approaches. One approach, already mentioned,
was simply to transfer an architectural idiom that
reeked of grandeur suggesting that, whatever
else, reform was a noble cause, as architects of
a later generation, though from a very different
angle, tried to express the nobility of the common
people in designs for the welfare state. Barry's
model of the Roman Palazzo Farnese, built by
the Farnese family, a new family whose wealth
was greatly increased when one of their number
became pope in the 1530s, gave a large central
space over which, London not sharing Rome's
climate, he sensibly put a roof. Around it, on both
levels, the walls are littered with portraits of the
heroes of reform, both the old toffs who, in the
manner of Lampedusa's Leopard, realised that
'things had to change if things were to stay the
same',[3] and the emerging plutocrats who wanted

a slice of the political power that had been reserved
for the aristocracy. It would have taken a particularly
single-minded early Victorian to argue that the burghers
of Manchester really deserved less parliamentary
representation than the two or three electors of Old
Sarum, under the unbending eye, even if only in effigy,
of Lord John Russell.

But the subtlest device Barry used on the interior of
the Reform Club also has the most elusive relationship
to political reform. What appears to be a large and solid
building occasionally melts into something less tangible.
The stairs from the main hall to the first-floor gallery, for
instance, have a mirror on the half landing, suggesting
an illusory space beyond. And above a fireplace on the
ground floor is a sheet of glass. A bust on the
mantelpiece and expectation of a flue behind imply it is a
mirror, except that rather than reflect the space back to
the observer, it actually gives a view into the dining room.
Reading these uncertain relationships as an analogue of
the outcome of reform would be too literal, but they do
make for an intriguing series of spaces where you could
never be sure your intrigues were entirely private.

This is the other side of club architecture. If a club's
purpose is either too obvious and familiar to need
expression, or its purpose is too elusive to lend itself to
expression, it can at least be designed to be a congenial
place where its members can engage enjoyably in the
designated purpose. Even during the 1970s, when
traditional clubland seemed destined for oblivion, the
new clubs that threatened to replace the hoary
established ones had to support social activity. Julyan
Wickham, who with his fellow architect Tchaik Chassay,
the wine merchant John Armit and confectionery heir
Tony Macintosh conceived several of the new
generation, including the Zanzibar in Covent Garden,
summarises the architectural challenge: 'It's how to
make a single, "buzzy" space,' he says, adding that
they often had 'horrible sites ... we had to work hard
to make something of them.'[4]

Opening in 1976, the Zanzibar offered its clientele
something between a saloon bar, restaurant and the
trendier nightclubs of the time such as Annabel's and
Tramp, in the era of punitive licensing laws and a tax
regime the strictures of which could be mitigated by
'legitimate' business expenses, like club memberships.
It was a single space orchestrated by Wickham and his
friends with a skill Barry would have respected. Along
one side was a bar the zigzag shape of which invited
conviviality, the indentations making natural groups
without the separation of booths or banquettes so that
conversation could flow without being forced. On the
other side were the dining tables, raised on a podium
so that the eye level of seated diners was the same as
that of standing drinkers, again an architectural device
intended to promote social contact in a way that might
be too intimate for a conventional restaurant. Again in

Lampedusa's own great-grandfather), frequently reflects on the words: 'If we want things to stay as they are, things will have to change.' These were first articulated by Fabrizio's nephew Tancredi (p 41), a supporter of Garibaldi's insurrection in Sicily in 1860 that triggered the Italian Risorgimento, and Fabrizio struggles to preserve his aristocratic position and privilege during the overthrow of the Bourbon kingdom of Naples and the rise of a new class of mafiosi, represented in the novel by Don Calogero Sedara.
4 Interview with the author.
5 Interview with the author.

Above
The lively face of the Electric House in Portobello Road, London, suggests more happens behind it than simple film-going.

Inset
Club area on the upper floor.

Opposite
Plans, Electric House.

Combining several different functions, and the restoration of an important historic building ... makes the architecture of Electric House rather more complicated. Its core is the Electric Cinema, designed by Valentin Seymour in 1910 as Britain's first purpose-built cinema, an extraordinary challenge to which he responded with a space that worked better for live music than recorded sound.

a way that Barry would have recognised, mirrors extended the illusion of space throughout, most notably turning a quadrant-shaped stage into an apparently circular one. However, unlike the Reform Club, *Playboy* never used it as a set for a photo shoot, though Jerry Hall posed, tastefully clad, for the publicity material.

London's social geography changed rapidly in the 1980s. The yuppies who forwent the suburbia of their parents to gentrify Camden and Islington often worked in media businesses in Soho, and a club to serve them had to borrow something from its neighbours such as the Colony Rooms and the Establishment, but with a dash of glamour and nostalgia. Tchaik Chassay, who designed Groucho's, the archetypal media-persons watering hole, explains that the models were the Algonquin, where Dorothy Parker honed her wit, crossed with an English country house. These influences, however, were expressed in a low key. Chassay himself calls the atmosphere 'reticent', adding that 'it was a big, rambling building with a character of its own'. The existing shell set the pattern for the spaces – 'it would be very exciting not to have an existing building, exhilarating not to be restrained', laments Chassay.[5]

The brightly lit, metal and glass bar faces the entrance from the vestibule and provides an immediate focus and invitation to use the space in a certain way. Beyond that, a dark carpet and unflashy furniture ensure that the space melts away into the background, towards a dining area at the back and a staircase to the first floor. The juxtapositions are too reticent to be incongruous, and the whole atmosphere seems to invite drinking and talking, even when almost empty. In these surroundings careers in journalism and television were made, just as Trollope's Phineas Finn was not the only ambitious young barrister whose frequent presence at the Reform Club gave his career a political twist.

Electric House in Portobello Road, one of London's newest clubs, continues the age-old club purpose of networking among people of similar interests, according to its architect Sasha Gebler. Combining several different functions, and the restoration of an important historic building, though, makes the architecture of Electric House rather more complicated. Its core is the Electric Cinema, designed by Valentin Seymour in 1910 as Britain's first purpose-built cinema, an extraordinary challenge to which he responded with a space that worked better for live music than recorded sound. By the late 1990s the numerous signatories to a petition bemoaning the derelict state of this important piece of film history, remembers Gebler, caused an unusually waggish planning officer to comment that if all the people who signed actually went there, it would never have sunk so low! But, as Gebler comments, the front of house was inadequate and a mezzanine inserted into the main space was 'horrible'.

It became clear that if the cinema were to reopen it would have to be in association with suitable amenities in adjoining premises. Fortunately the owner, Monsoon's Peter Simon, had both the will and deep enough pockets to acquire a scruffy supermarket next door, and brought in Soho House as operator. What emerged was a composite institution of a cinema, a restaurant and a club with a ready-made theme and purpose, deriving directly from the cinema. A new three-storey building with a narrow glass front on to Portobello Road, which wraps in an L-shape around the cinema, houses the new facilities, the brasserie on the ground floor and club above.

Electric House adds a neat twist to the relationship between clubs and architecture. If most clubs start with a social purpose and graduate to architecture, Electric House started with the wish to preserve a historic building and established a club to preserve it. Though the new architecture treats Seymour's design respectfully, it also deliberately reveals the social activity within. In this it is the mirror image of another club that has a distinct purpose, a strictly controlled membership and no premises whatsoever. It is called the Architecture Club. ᴐ

The Commonwealth Club, London

Eleanor Curtis explains how, in 1998, the Commonwealth Club undertook a redesign to attract a broader and younger membership.

Founded over a hundred years ago, the Royal Commonwealth Society (RCS) has existed to promote a 'wider understanding of the nature of the Commonwealth and its people'. It is the charity responsible for the members' club once known as the Royal Commonwealth Club and now simply known as the Commonwealth Club.

The club itself has always had an advantageous location, being in the heart of central London off Trafalgar Square, and is widely known amongst diplomatic circles both past and present. Owned and run by the RCS, it once occupied a whole string of buildings on Northumberland Avenue, offering all the essential elements of a traditional gentleman's club. The smoking rooms, reading rooms, lounges and bedrooms were typically adorned with various furs, masks and horns collected from the far corners of the Commonwealth, and large heavy portraits of HRH Elizabeth II and other VIPs. However, due to financial restructuring the society sold off a significant chunk of its prime real estate to fund a modern refurbishment

Opposite, top
The lower ground floor has
re-used the original walnut
panelling to give the lounge
its traditional feel.

Opposite, bottom
The dining hall with the
suspended glass dining room
at the mezzanine level.
Primary colours have been
used throughout reflecting
the club's corporate identity.

Above left
The glass-encased entrance
with its mandarin stone gives
a glimpse into the main dining
hall with the suspended glass
bubble.

Above right
The original clock face design
by Sir Herbert Baker now
hangs in the main dining hall,
suspended from steel rods
housed in glass, and can
be viewed from the street.

of its club, retaining a mere 20 per cent of its
original square footage, but in the original
building. The new club opened in 1998.

Designer Linda Morey Smith was
commissioned to give the club a fresh feel,
in order to attract a younger membership and
put it back on the map. The 'Royal' was even
taken out of its title to encourage a more open
attitude towards membership. The logo was
also updated to give the club a new corporate
image – a splash of primary colours dragged
across the palette.

The complete makeover of this 'self-
confessed conservative organisation' has been
described by commentators as a 'brave piece of
interior architecture'. Whilst retaining the solid
traditional values of this historic club through
the reuse of the original walnut wall panelling
at the lower ground-floor level lounges, Morey
Smith was able to introduce some modern
architectural concepts to the restricted site.

The main entrance off Northumberland Avenue
is floored with mandarin stone and encased in
frameless glass, providing a view of the main dining
area with its mezzanine gallery.

The party piece is the floating dining room – a glass
bubble suspended above the main dining hall, which
serves as a private dining room, accessible from the
mezzanine bar level. The coloured chairs of the main
dining hall complement the primary colours of the
club's identity – red, green and blue in big curves on
straight backs.

The original Sir Herbert Baker clock face has been
rehoused in glass and is suspended from stainless-
steel rods – a contemporary housing for such a
traditional object and club icon – at the front of the
dining hall where it can also be viewed from the street
outside.

The revamp has clearly worked. The club is now
packed with a mix of young and old, and there is a buzz
to the atmosphere more akin to a busy bar/ restaurant
than a traditional conservative royal club. Δ

The Core Club

New York

The London-based interdisciplinary practice Universal Design Studio has been asked by the Core Group to develop ideas for a new private members' club in New York. **Jonathan Clarke**, a director at Universal, describes how the brief for the Core Club has been made all the more complicated by the established history of the club environment in New York, making the project a challenging but ultimately highly rewarding task.

The basis of the development of the Core Club was that it should be exclusive and unique without obvious references to the gentleman's club model. The founder of the Core Group, Jennie Saunders, has an extensive background in the development and management of luxury lifestyle companies, having begun with the creation of an urban country-club concept in 1990, which through several strategic alliances ultimately became the Reebok Sports Club/NY and the Sports Club/LA facilities. The brief from Saunders both expanded the options available to Universal as architects and designers and imposed an intriguing constraint that demanded a tight interaction throughout the design process between the design itself and the development of a unique combination of services.

The exclusivity of the private members' club has generally been confined only to the membership process. In this way, business-class lounges, an example of a members' club more akin to everyday contemporary experience, are more obviously dependent simply on the ability to purchase entry. However, the membership offering is rarely unique. Within the private members' club, the architecture of the spaces may be

Above
Library/lounge for the
Core Club, New York.

slick, comfortable and individual but the members are a captive audience who often benefit only from extended licensing hours and the status that membership brings. In addition, many private clubs offer membership based upon profession and status. Although generally not pitched in this manner, this is the distilled result of the nomination process. The notion of exclusivity within this programme type becomes less of an architectural or design problem and more about a perceived quality driven by styling.

Universal has undertaken the development of a design process that builds on the complexity of the initial brief. Having explored the typology of the private club extensively, what became apparent and seemed ultimately of most significance was the uniqueness of the proposed combination of services the Core Club was to offer. The assembled service consultants for this new development on East 55th Street represented the best of their individual professions. The notion of the club as a desirable destination was vitally underpinned by the quality and essence of its

individual components. The Core Club would function as a personally comprised community of individuals with the best of what cities have to offer readily available. Like a city, the elements are individually complex and ultimately will have an inherent flexibility.

It became apparent to Universal that the goal needed to be much more than the physical construction of a notion of exclusivity. Of course, the Core Club will have all of the elements associated with the traditional members' club, but the carefully selected, individual and complex levels of service and content will allow members to define individual experiences. As design professionals it is in the design of the spaces and structure of the club, in response to these service elements, that Universal Design Studio provides the true understanding. It has the ability to work across disciplines and to understand where consultants can really aid the delivery of a special project.

The architecture will be unique and dynamic. The membership process will allude to exclusivity, and the services on offer will be of a quality and type that, combined, make them entirely new. The success of the club will only be realised with the fusing of all of these elements. ∆

High Club

Nigel Coates in Conversation
with Eleanor Curtis

The first essays of the very first publication of the *AA Files* (of the Architectural Association, London) in 1982, were on clubs. Architect Nigel Coates, then known as the *enfant terrible* of the AA school and founder of the group and publication *Narrative Architecture Today* (NATO) wrote one of these essays, entitled 'New Clubs at Large'. It opens:

> Ephemeral, gratuitous and hardly ever a serious job for the hard-nut designer, nightclubs are the vaudeville of the city stage. Yet clubs, places of nocturnal entertainment, have always been a social safety valve for turning transgressive forces loose – Berlin in the 30s, Paris in the 50s and now London and New York. Nightclubs anticipate and encourage the spectacle of the self, and in doing so they emphasise many of the more general issues which architecture must include if meaning is to have anything to do with the sensuous faculties of the body.

And goes on:

> Nightclubs ... have little or no exterior significance other than their actual nameplates – innuendos like 'Legends', 'Floozies', 'Heaven', etc. Invariably hidden beneath ordinary city buildings, these clubs take on the project of the night by burying themselves. Underground they are free to promote what rarely could happen in the streets, to give a contrived reality to what would otherwise be unlikely, taboo, or at best occasional. Inside, environments are designed to intoxicate, confuse, and play up the theatricality of mass showmanship.

This idea of the underground, subterranean, hidden world of nightclubs of the 1980s, a world that emerges with the onset of night amongst an otherwise familiar cityscape, has evolved into the 21st century with a very different energy. Coates's nightclubs of the 1980s were about

expression of the self in a theatrical, almost circus-like environment, where architecture could be pushed into thinking about the possible interactions that the physical space could have with the sensuous body. Nightclubs were places to experiment with your own identity, encouraged by the deliberate confusion of the interior environment.

Twenty years on from that article, London is seeing the evolution of the nightclub from this hidden underground club concerned with the spectacle of the self, to a sort of hybrid bar-lounge-club. This new hybrid, which may be open almost 24 hours, and which affords different activities in different zones, also follows the night-and-day rhythms of the real world. Clubbers have moved up a floor or two, occupying the lobbies of trendsetting hotels and cool bars, with resident DJs to hand mixing the grooves and setting the tune. Names are becoming familiar as nightclubs establish a reputation that is then stamped on to a chain of clubs. Some nightclubs, such as Chinawhite (see later), are also joining the branding game.

Nightclubbing can be reduced to its core elements of music, dance, dress and drink (and sometimes drugs). However, a club is more than the sum of its parts. Nightclubs are about ambience and identity, and the clubs that house the clubbers do not have to be architecturally sophisticated to be successful. Some of the most interesting and thriving clubs can be quite grotty outside and in.

The nightclub equation is a balance between the people the club attracts and the activities they do in the club to bring the place alive, in turn encouraged (or discouraged) by the interior space. Clubbers are attracted to a particular club in the first place typically because of the identity it emulates. The 'identity' in this case is hard to define, as it is interdependent with the type of people who come to the place. However, this 'identity' does not appear from nowhere: there are elements of design – whether grand or grunge – that make it a 'happening' space, and these can be as subtle as lighting effects or as obvious as refitting the entire interior. But at the end of the day, it is the interaction of

Previous spread (detail)
Branson Coates Architecture's Taxim nightclub in Istanbul, 1991.

Above
Nigel Coates of Branson Coates Architecture, professor of architecture at the Royal College of Art, London.

Right
Spread from Coates's latest book (and project), *Ecstacity*.

Sketch, London
A collaborative venture led by restaurateur Mourad Mazouz and designed by Noe Duchaufour Lawrence, Sketch transforms a Neo-Palladian house in London's West End into a design fantasy in which two restaurants, two bars and a patisserie are all given very different design treatments.

Below, top and bottom left
During the day, The Gallery offers an art gallery with audio-visual displays by different artists, and by the evening transforms into a restaurant.

Below, top right
The lecture room. Reds, oranges, pinks and gold are used in contrast to the minimalist blacks and whites of other rooms for this fine-dining restaurant.

Below, bottom right
The pod-like toilets of the East Bar, as reflected in the glass dome.

the clubbers with these spaces, as Coates hinted at 20 years ago, that makes a nightclub thrive.

I went back to Nigel Coates in June 2003, 20 years after his comments in 'New Clubs at Large', and asked him about his own views on the ways nightclubs have changed. Working as an architect with Doug Branson, as Branson Coates Architecture, Coates was also responsible for a number of bars and clubs in the late 1980s and early 1990s.

NC: 'I think clubs have become an established arena for finding a match between your own identity and aspirations for identity, and for being able to experiment and explore. In the early 1980s there were relatively few clubs around that came from the idea of the club as being a parade ground for the way you looked, your friends and the importance of dance. There were clubs like the Embassy and later Blitz, but there were also all those clubs that were formed around punk, which were

really shabby places, often just colonised. Clubs would become identifiable places that would be associated with a whole kind of generational and particular identity, to do with certain kinds of music and lifestyle.

'You dressed the way that went with the music and some people dressed more extremely than others, but it was these places where groups could test their boundaries. This included those people who would get it and to some extent, be indifferent to those people who didn't. The notion of exclusivity was much more dynamic than simply signing up to be a member. As far as I can remember, nobody at those times was a member. It was tacit. It was to do with whether you were attracted to it or not and whether you were a good match for the other people. I think that's an interesting model as to how a club might form.

'Since then, clubs have become big business and they've become trophy entities that can make a lot of money and have been adopted by huge corporations. They range from Disneyland on the one hand, which has

'Sketch is one of those types of clubs that is in itself a city. It has the variety of a city and sections within it, and changes from day to day and day to night and so on, to try to grasp different groups of people.'

actually had its own club village attached to its various theme parks, through to the other extreme – where an individual entrepreneur might see a gap in the market and simply rent a space or come to some deal about a space that in itself was not really nightclub oriented at all. These are two extremes that run in parallel.

'And of course club culture, instead of being for those experimental few, is pervasive. Everybody, including every teenager, aspires to go to the local club. At the age of 14 or 15, the club is a potentially good place for young people to test themselves, to exchange ideas, meet people and be a forum – being a forum in the Roman sense. A forum is not disconnected, a forum never had a fence around it, a forum had a sort of osmotic relationship with the rest of the city and people would come together …

'But clubbing has become a kind of very commercial thing. There are a lot of clubs in London like Fabric and Heaven that are still bashing on, owned by successful entrepreneurs or entrepreneurial companies who see them as good in their portfolio along with restaurants and the rest of the leisure industry.'

The 'big business' nightclubs that Coates refers to are now assimilated into London's West End club culture (for example Chinawhite and Fabric – see later), with the fewer experimental clubs hovering more around the city's edges in the east and south (where venues are more available and affordable). Money is being made and the club entrepreneur has taken advantage of the popularity of a club that offers more than a dance floor by situating these clubs in the basement of a restaurant or depositing a DJ amongst the tables halfway through dinner. Clubs are also becoming more specialised, offering very particular environments within which to explore.

Coates sees the design of the club as a facilitator to the success and life of the club itself. He cites London's hybrid club Sketch (which opened in early 2003) as embodying where some of the top-end elegant clubs are heading.

NC: 'As a society we've got experience. We've become professional at being clubbers. We start younger. There is more information about what each club represents. You go, you try it and if you have a good time you might go again. But I think that club culture in its broadest sense applies pretty much to all young people – it doesn't have a marginal nature. There will be other more special, more particular clubs, like Club Khali, for example, which has an Indian connection with experimental modern Indian dance music and boys dressed in saris, cross-dressing with a global multicultural feel, and a global spectacle.

'Gay clubs, which are specialised places, can sometimes be rough and might need to have a sort of military, dungeonesque or even harsh environment because that sets the scene for what the punters are

Sketch, London

Opposite, top
The West Bar is a long room with a glazed ceiling. The white terrazzo floor folds up to form a long bar. Furnished with a mixture of reupholstered 1970s chairs, it is open during the day, serving food at lunch time.

Opposite, bottom
In the East Bar, Sketch is at its most futuristic and most nostalgic. The bar is accommodated in a round egg UFO-like form. Two staircases around this structure lead to the toilets that are housed in 12 separate pods. The East Bar is the most intimate and exclusive space. It is open in the evenings only to those who have table reservations, or are members or on the guest list.

Above left
The Parlour. This café/patisserie offers sumptuous cakes displayed like jewels in a cabinet. Behind the display cabinets there are glimpses of a man and woman having high tea printed on the wallpaper.

Above right
The staircase leading up to the lecture room with chocolate pouring down the steps, using a thick raised paint to create an 'oozing' effect.

after – which is basically each other. On the other hand there are going to be elegant places like Sketch, for example, which you could loosely define as a club. It is very exclusive and very affiliated with the fashion and art worlds. It uses design at a very high-pitched level. But in the end, even at that hyper-pitched level, if the people in it don't go beyond the club itself and be more fascinating and more, let's say, in command of the environment, then it doesn't work. The design has got to be a facilitator.'

Sketch comprises the functions of two restaurants, two bars, a patisserie, lecture room and library, with some rooms doubling up in use. Created by Mourad Mazouz, director of nearby MoMo (on Heddon Street), Sketch hosts objects by known designers such as Ron Arad and Chris Levine in carefully crafted interiors. Rooms double up to offer different functions at different times of the day: the Gallery, which hosts art shows from 10am, opens as a restaurant at 7pm and transforms into a lounge-bar after 11pm as the volume of the music is increased and the furniture shifted for lounging. Toilets for the bars are contained in human-sized eggs and toilets for the library and lecture room are adorned with crystals sponsored by Swarovski. Sketch's own press releases describe the club as 'a project that will constantly evolve, like a painting that never dries'.

NC: 'Sketch is going for a fairly broad clientele. It's open in the daytime – to anybody – to go and look at the art work. To go there in the evening you need to make a reservation, but you don't have to be a member. Sketch is one of those types of clubs that is in itself a city. It has the variety of a city and sections within it, and changes from day to day and day to night and so on, to try to grasp different groups of people.'

In the mid- to late 1980s, Branson Coates designed a few 'loungey, exclusive environments' in Japan that had a clubby atmosphere. Their very first restaurant, the Metropole, had connotations of a gentleman's club, set up in such a way as to give people the feeling that they were in a much grander environment than was actually the case. The firm's only nightclub was in Istanbul; Taxim, designed in 1991, was situated in a large old factory, with the appropriate connotations of decay, in a run-down but very central part of the city. The space was vast – 3,000 square metres – with a restaurant, two or three bars and a gigantic double-height dance floor. Branson Coates designed into it many unexpected links between these elements, with the idea that on entering the club would be revealed bit by bit rather than being presented all at once, just as the city reveals itself at unexpected moments.

NC: 'The spaces [in Taxim] would be revealed slowly as you got to feel comfortable in the different parts [of the club] and then felt more experimental to go and explore further.

'Rather than the way that a lot of people think about buildings, houses, spaces where there is a defined mood to each room, there was a lot of linkage in those spaces. There were walkways that cut across spaces and a walkway behind the bar, next to the big restaurant. You could go behind the bar, walk along a raised walkway that went over the top of the loos, that looked down into the loos, and then you would find yourself in the middle of the dance floor. Even at the time, we talked about it as a microcosm of the city and the client called it a night park. In terms of its structure it had a lot of intersections, an aspect to cities I've always found so fascinating, and that is reflected in the way we wanted people to feel. Perhaps people might go there for dinner and somehow be drawn into crossing some kind of mental boundary, which meant they discovered they were suddenly in some other situation and perhaps would start to behave in a slightly different way. It was about self-discovery and multiplicity.

'One of the great things I have always believed about cities is that you are constantly taken into moments of the unexpected which can actually make you jump tracks, and that this possibility of a chance encounter or a previously unexperienced relationship to some situation is fundamental to the attraction of cities. It might be in a space but it might be with people. On the one hand you might have people who meet who know each other, but then there are the other sorts of moments – flash moments – when you pass somebody in the street and you recognise them or you find them attractive, and they look at you ... I think it's very interesting the fact that a lot of places that stimulate attraction – mutual attraction – are often quite rough and ready and undesigned, and sometimes really trashy, on the inside as well as the outside.'

Coates's current project, Ecstacity, is the evolution of some of the ideas established 20 years ago at the AA, which develops the notion of the city as a multilayered, multidimensional place of many spaces that shapes and challenges our daily experiences. It is about how the city works in, and with, time, and the interaction between social and individual perceptions of what the city actually is. The city, in this sense, has things in common with a nightclub.

Fabric, London

Below
Dance Floor 2 has a DJ box to the side of the stage and a VIP balcony looking on from the left.

Opposite
The VIP lounge looking over the main dance floor.

NC: 'I wouldn't say it was as crude as looking at the whole city as though it were a nightclub but there is a relationship between them, because it is acknowledging the fact that a city is multiterritory and multiread; that the same place can be read by different people in entirely different ways. Camden Market, for example, is probably read by different people in different ways, so is Old Compton Street, so is Portobello Road and Golborne Road. Each place is a kind of a club, in a curious way, which is inhabited. Golborne Road, for example, is inhabited by five or six different ethnic groups simultaneously and out of that it produces an amazing frisson about what a city is for everybody concerned.

'The Ecstacity project started in 1990 with a show at the Architectural Association in which it looked quite formally at what makes up a city. All these ideas were extended to a hypothetical city which I called Ecstacity.

'We defined the relationship between the city and the user of the city. For example, I think Venice is an ecstatic place and not just because it's pretty but because its extraordinary condition creates all sorts of feelings in exploring it, which make you reconsider other places. It is sexy, desirous, furtive and exquisitely beautiful.

'Whereas Ecstacity is not necessarily beautiful, it's got everything from grungy old markets through to heroic new buildings. Firstly, I had to conceive the nature of the city and from that came this idea of taking pieces from other cities and intertwining them so that it would accentuate what really is London.

'London is essentially a 19th-century city but now it contains so many different races and cultures. I find it fascinating the way they interweave and in certain

'One of the great things I have always believed about cities is that you are constantly taken into moments of the unexpected which can actually make you jump tracks, and that this possibility of a chance encounter or a previously unexperienced relationship to some situation is fundamental to the attraction of cities. It might be in a space but it might be with people.'

city, how the activities in a city are intrinsically connected to the fabric of the city, and about how the city is as we know it now. I was looking at how a sample area of Trafalgar Square to St Paul's, and to the north bank of the Thames, could go a step further in stimulating the exchange between spaces and people. It would build on what was there and stretch the idea of a single building or a single place, with an iconic facade or a kind of iconic identity, and look at how that could be drawn out using new architectural elements to create a kind of fibre that interlinked. There were functional walkways that served to connect bits that were otherwise unconnected, like a garden to a bridge, for example the gardens of the north Embankment to Waterloo Bridge. This created a different reading of yourself in relation to the places take on a clear identity that you could lasso and say it is club-like. But in other parts it is ambivalent and both defined and undefined. This enabled me through the technique of the guide – the type of book which is a guide to a city – to lay the ground of exploring this place, hopefully in a way that was fresh, like any guide book. It was a starting point to try to create a book that was layered and in itself would be like a city. Or in a way like a club. If you "get it", then you are in it, and if you don't "get it", it will be a complete mystery.'

The book Ecstacity, published in September 2003, is simultaneously a novel, a guide, a book about cities, a book about architecture and a book about people and sensibilities. The idea of the "guide book" was used as a useful tool to ground this complexity and give it structure. However, the essence of Ecstacity is the interactions between the people and the spaces – just as the life and success of a nightclub is dependent on that interaction.

'London is essentially a 19th-century city but now it contains so many different races and cultures. I find it fascinating the way they interweave and in certain places take on a clear identity that you could lasso and say it is club-like. But in other parts it is ambivalent and both defined and undefined.'

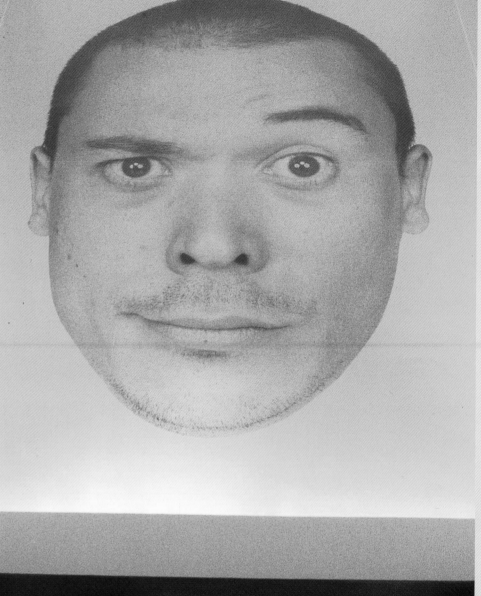

Light Bar, London

Opposite and above
Different coloured lighting affects are enhanced with the use of overhead audio-visual art displays.

NC: 'We have started off talking about how the environment, or the buildings that make up an environment, hint at something more than just a pragmatic reading or an aesthetic reading of what they are. They should stimulate. Without that sort of partnership with experience they don't really have much use. It is the same for nightclubs, in that whoever is setting up a nightclub has to be able to anticipate the way people are going to behave in that environment. There is a level of design – even if a club is in an old railway arch with one single light bulb and a huge sound system and a load of illegal beer – but there is still something being designed in the concept that is actually kind of put into effect.

'There is a nightclub in these extraordinary arches underneath the railway viaducts north of London's King's Cross, which for years have been an experimental ground for clubs. It's quite interesting, because there are five arches with openings between them, I think a couple or two or three bars along the length of them, with different music in each arch, and then each one has a kind of exit to a little patio area that's extended in the front, so when you go to it you see all these people behind these bushes that are in their little enclosures for each of these five arches.

'It has a kind of continental feel as an environment because of its outside space. As with lots of clubs in Italy or France that have huge outdoor spaces, there's a real mix of people and it's this slightly Eurotrash, slightly gay, grungy space that is very successful.'

In contrast, London has also witnessed the emergence of a very different sort of club, one which is heavy on design and image, a financial success story, and carries international stature. At the other end of the scale to one-off experimental clubs in the dis-used arches of King's Cross, or the basements of Hoxton Square, are the large heaving nightclubs in the West End of London. This is clubbing on a mass scale with big profits as its goal.

Chinawhite, London

Right and below
Both hard and soft furnishings, including tents, are used to create an Eastern flavour to the club.

Chinawhite is one of these success stories, sold on its image as an Asian-themed members' nightclub with top DJs spinning sounds for the socialites and celebrities of the day. The Indonesian-born designer Satmoko Ball fused Bali/Java/Sumatra styles and developed an intimate space through low ceilings and attention to oriental details. Chinawhite has almost become emblematic of London's (even the UK's) club culture. It has created a reputation that attracts top-name celebrities, and is widely cited in celebrity columns and the popular press across the globe. Chinawhite is also opening a club in Moscow that will epitomise British culture and sophistication for eager Muscovites. What is, in essence, a night-time experience has evolved to become almost a model for club-life throughout the Western world.

Other London venues that have played on their oriental inspirations to attract the crowds include the Funky Buddha, MoMo and the Cinnamon Club. Not all of those cited here are nightclubs, but they are part of the new 'fusion' of bar, restaurant, lounge, with resident DJ and a dedicated dancing crowd – and all are very successful in establishing a strong identity in a city heaving with club competition. Both MoMo and the Cinnamon Club also reserve areas for members only, increasing the desirability of these clubs with this touch of exclusivity.

Fabric is another of London's big club stories but in a very different style to Chinawhite. It is housed in a converted Victorian storage building, heading towards Clerkenwell on the City's Charterhouse Street (away from London's West End). The interior design has maintained many of the old fixtures including piping, raw brick and odd metalwork, with enormous internal windows. The club is divided into three rooms, all with its mix of cutting-edge sounds from drum-and-bass to deep house, and beyond to chill-out with its low seating and comfy chairs. Door policies restrict entrance to non-suit-wearing clubbers only – the antithesis of London's golden-oldie clubs like Stringfellow's or Annabel's.

Another type of informal club that has sold itself on its identity as defined by its design is the hotel lobbies of London. Some have a named designer attached to them, like the Prada shop in New York is like a club, although only a brand. Gucci or Prada also signify a kind of club that you belong to if you wear the clothes, or if you know a lot about the merchandise. And there is also Top Shop, which is like a club in that it has loud music and people are encouraged to feel relaxed.

'There is an idea that an environment could be two things at once, that it could have a certain straightforward function but then it could adopt nuances of other places or other conditions ... I'm arguing in all this for more slippage, more crossover, more exaggeration, between inside and outside, between the hot and cold, the soft and the hard, the new and the old.'

Referring to the hybrid club Sketch in central London, Coates expands on his idea of the playfulness of architecture.

'There is an idea that an environment could be two things at once, that it could have a certain straightforward function but then it could adopt nuances of other places or other conditions ... I'm arguing in all this for more slippage, more crossover, more exaggeration, between inside and outside, between the hot and cold, the soft and the hard, the new and the old.'

three Philippe Starck bars: the Light Bar at the St Martin's Lane Hotel in Covent Garden with its multicoloured light effects; the Long Bar at the Sanderson Hotel near Oxford Circus, another theatrical creation with beautiful lighting set amongst an oasis-garden backdrop; and the extravagant second bar, the Purple Bar, at the Sanderson Hotel. Other hotel bars are simply cool and elegant, for example the Met Bar at the Metropole Hotel, Park Lane (members only) and the Mandarin Bar at the Mandarin Oriental Hyde Park. Whilst strictly bars and not clubs, these establishments create a club-like atmosphere whether through their exclusive door policies or via the select bunch of people who go there. Music is also a key feature and along with the lounge idea, enhances the club-like atmosphere.

Perhaps the idea of a club can be pushed even further, beyond the hotel lobbies and DJ-hosted restaurants, to shops and supermarkets. Coates makes the important point about dress code and logos that can create the idea of belonging, out of very little else.

NC: 'We are also seeing shops becoming clubs and clubs emerging in perhaps much looser, more experimental ways. For example, the

NC: 'Going back to Sketch, I think it encourages playfulness, in a sense that there are unexpected environments, like the toilets inside the eggs or the sheer scale of the video room and the input of the music in that space where it is becoming unreal. It is like an extension of your mind and your experience but at the same time it is stimulating you because you can't predict what's actually going to come up. It's not genuinely interactive in the technological sense but it does offer contrasts and evolutions.

'There are all these different moods [at Sketch] which are ostensibly separated but all interlink. It seems to me to produce the frisson between these various conditions, as opposed to, say, the Madonna Inn or Schrager Hotel which tend to offer many moods but when you are in each one there is no real questioning about what is going on outside ... In other words it's commercialised and sort of banalised. It's all prepared for you. I don't think the Schrager Hotel is as successful at encapsulating a sense of experiment for the people that are using these places, as it might be. They're are too aesthetic in a way. Even so, I think Philippe Starck's work is fantastically important in all those areas where there are connotations of sexuality, of elegance, of kitsch, of a certain playfulness.'

And Chinawhite?

NC: 'That's a bit of a theme park isn't it?' △D

Note
1 Nigel Coates, *Ecstacity*, Laurence King (London), 2003.

The Democratiser:
A Conversation with
David Adjaye

David Adjaye of Adjaye Associates is the designer of one of London's most popular nightclubs, or DJ bars, The Social. Launched some four years ago, The Social is still reaping the awards (in 2002 it was *Time Out* DJ Bar of the Year). Since re-forming his studio in 2000, Adjaye has embarked on a new TV career as presenter of the BBC3 contemporary design show 'Dreamspaces' (alongside Charlie Luxton and Justine Frischmann, former lead singer with Elastica). Contiguous, but seemingly antithetical to Adjaye's meteoric rise in London's fashionable design world, has been his determination to move his architectural practice on from the froth of small commercial schemes to more serious civic community projects and international prize commissions, such as that for the Oslo Nobel Peace Center. Here, he discusses with **Helen Castle** DJ bars, club culture and his insistence on an architecture of spatial democracy.

As a great believer in the democratisation of space, David Adjaye is ambivalent about the notion of clubs per se, which tend by their very nature to be spatially exclusive or hierarchical. When designing his DJ bar, The Social, in the West End of London, for Heavenly Records in 1999, he intentionally set out to create an inviting atmosphere on a domestic scale. (On Little Portland Street, just off Upper Regent Street, the bar occupies a narrow, deep site at basement and ground-floor levels that was previously a strip joint.)

Conceived as a 'home from home' for an established social group at the record company, The Social was to provide a permanent place to party, with a serious bar. The notion was to widen rather than narrow the net of an existing social scene. Its exterior and entrance were intentionally designed to negate the convention of the nightclub queue. Thus the street facade provides transparency, with a steel-and-glass screen that can be slid back when desired. There are also glass bricks in the ceiling and floor of the tunnel, which runs from the street entrance

to the rear sauna-like bar/dining area on the ground floor and connects with the stairs to the main basement bar. The tunnel is constructed as a 'holder', creating a sense of something to come for the visitor. Rather than barring or exempting people it is designed to invite them in, providing with its thresholds tantalising glimpses of the main spaces.

In conversation, Adjaye likens his scheme for The Social to a 'deli among supermarkets'. Built at the end of the 1990s it was a pioneering 'designed' DJ bar that foreshadowed the demise of the large-scale corporate super-clubs – a trend he charted in his dedicated feature on nightclubs, 'Clubbed to Death', for the spring season of 'Dreamspaces'.[1] The watershed for this shift in the nightclub genre came with the closure of Home in 2001. Though the seven-storey super-club in Leicester Square was opened the same year as The Social, it survived for a mere two years. The trend away from big and brash spaces has reverberated throughout the UK, with the scaling down of Cream in Liverpool and Gatecrasher in Sheffield. As Adjaye explains in the programme: 'People haven't stopped going out and they still want to hear loud music, but they want to hear

Previous page
David Adjaye of Adjaye Associates.

Previous spread, below and opposite
Adjaye & Russell Architecture & Design, The Social, London, 1999.

it in more intimate personal spaces that are really designed. They don't want to go to places that are bland and corporate. If the 1990s were about the super-club, then this is the decade of the DJ bar. At first they were just pubs with decks in, but DJ bars have become a third space that is neither a pub nor club. The design is often as much of a draw as the tunes.'[2]

To illustrate this point, 'Dreamspaces' visited three clubs in addition to The Social, all with very different architectural treatments: Cargo, designed by Jamie Fobert, inhabits a series of brick arches in London's East End; NASA is a pure white revisitation of *2001* in Copenhagen, and was designed by Johannes Torpes; and Rehab in Leeds, with its swanky futuristic design and cheeky medical references by Soo Wilkinson, bridges the gap between DJ bar and super-club.

A key development of the specially commissioned DJ bars is the way that they incorporate a 'multiple set of experiences' under a single roof. Adjaye explains how The Social clients required that it should bring eating,

'If the 1990s were about the super-club, then this is the decade of the DJ bar. At first they were just pubs with decks in, but DJ bars have become a third space that is neither a pub nor club. The design is often as much of a draw as the tunes.'

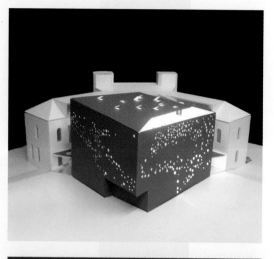

Above
Concept model for the Nobel Peace Center in Oslo. Located in the old railway station of Vestbanen, the centre is to be situated opposite Oslo City Hall where the Nobel Peace Ceremony takes place in December each year. By presenting the past and present laureates and their work, the centre is intended to meet the public appetite for further information and discussion on topics surrounding the Nobel Prize.

Opposite
The Idea Store in Whitechapel Road, east London, is one of two Idea Stores that have been commissioned from Adjaye Associates by the London borough of Tower Hamlets, with four additional libraries planned. The Idea Store is a redefinition of the neighbourhood library. It is intended to increase the use of local library facilities through the creation of a high-quality environment that is more akin to people's experience of retail than public services. Produced in partnership with Tower Hamlets College, the store will combine state-of-the-art facilities with resource learning areas for educational purposes. Provision will also be made on site for retail and café facilities. With both Idea Stores currently on site, the Chrisp Street location will open in January 2004 and the flagship on Whitechapel Road in the autumn of 2004. The Idea Store in Whitechapel Road was part of the exhibition on projects that are changing the world at the 2002 Venice Biennale.

drinking and hearing music together in a single place, 'without traipsing around London in the rain'.[3] This has meant that evening after evening this small venue has had to survive a long night. The impact of this, however, was built in and The Social was designed with 'behaviour-driven materials'; the concrete seats and tables in the downstairs bar are more akin to street or park furniture than those usually found in a bar or restaurant. Adjaye likens the environment to Trinidad, where the best parties take place in the intimate and durable setting of people's back yards.

Despite its ruggedness and now slightly worn edges, The Social, in terms of its hybridisation of space, has much in common with a new clutch of clubs that have begun to emerge, such as Sketch and the New York members' club by Universal Design Studio (see Jonathan Clarke's 'The Core Club, New York', on pp 76–77). Adjaye elaborates that Sketch is a journey into Mourad Mazouz's mind, with 'something distinctly alien going on at the back' (he is referring here to the UFO-shaped East bar that is audaciously

suspended in the middle of an 18th-century room). It is a 'cut and paste' without spatial sequence. Despite the money thrown at it, Sketch lacks the architectural coherence of The Social, which provides turngates for different moments allowing a visual flow between the independent spaces. Adjaye's obvious enjoyment of the fantastical elements of Sketch are here underscored by a serious critique.

As Adjaye points out, the hierarchy of spaces that exists at Sketch inevitably result in a lack of democracy. (The Parlour or patisserie at the front of the building is open all day to the public, but in the evening the club, with its two bars, is open only to those with a table reservation or those privileged enough to be members or on the guest list. The main eating area in the Lecture Room and Library area is prohibitively expensive at approximately £200 a head, and has been the subject of much speculation in the press.[4] Without membership or a place on the guest list, the public can only buy themselves into the most prestigious spaces.)

This can be perceived to be indicative of broader currents in contemporary life, in which the general push for financial success has replaced the type of exciting subversive and often subterranean spaces that Nigel Coates described in his article in *AA Files* 20 years ago (see 'Nightclubbing: Nigel Coates in Conversation with Eleanor Curtis', pp 78–89). With even younger people tending to be aspirational in their desires, a viable counterculture has effectively been eroded. For Adjaye this reflects a wider collapse in self-identity. Whereas the vibrant New Romantic club scene of the 1980s placed an emphasis on individual creativity and often home-produced or customised outfits, 'people's desires are now driven by association with an image. It becomes a relief to people that they belong to Soho House or the Babington set. Raped of style by the likes of Galliano, people have effectively become branded.' Adjaye sees this as all part of a new shift towards curating in retail and consumption, as there is a general erosion of people's confidence with them simply not knowing what they want. In stores such as Collette in Paris and Corsi Como in Milan, the edit is done for the customer. Thus the power of interior design has become the power to curate space. Rather than being about a series of details, it is about the ability to control mood.

I am interested whether the type of skills that Adjaye has acquired through his finely honed, commercial spaces such as The Social and Browns Focus store in Mayfair are directly transferable to his civic and public works. Could the notion of targeting a particular audience, which is so integral to club design, be directly translatable into the public sector? Adjaye makes it clear that for a public work, architectural provision has to be about a lot more than style. The Idea Stores that he is designing as a series of new libraries for east London

Notes
1 'Dreamspaces', episode five,
15 April 2003.
2 Ibid.
3 Ibid.
4 This expansion of the
analysis of the spaces at
Sketch is my own rather than
Adjaye's. For reviews
of Sketch, see Jay Rayner in
the *Guardian*, 11 January 2003:
'To say the gastronomic
restaurant at Sketch – called
the Lecture Room – is
expensive, is a little like saying
Dolly Parton is a big girl. It is
nose-bleedingly expensive.'
On 9 February 2003, Larry
Elliot in the *Observer* cited
Sketch to support his
argument that consumer
spending can only go down.

are 'a fiction – a place where you delight in information. This is not sci-fi. They have to provide an infrastructure that transcends the sort of life cycle of five years of a club.' But how can it be possible to target youth without delivering the sort of branded design that they are accustomed to in the media? Adjaye is convinced that it can, and should be, a lot more subtle than stylistic imitation. It is a matter of finding a 'sensibility' that goes towards both rigour and slackness. There has to be the same balance between the formal and casual that is being played out in the younger generation. This can be physically expressed in architecture by 'the heightening and collapsing of materials and details'.

If, as is suggested by Adjaye's observations on design and its audience, the current draw to club culture is associated with an insecure craving to belong to a top-dog set, we could well be in for a period of readjustment. This may come in the form of an economic ebb and an associated decline in consumer spending, or even a polarisation of politics as happened under Margaret Thatcher in the 1980s. However, what is clear is that despite his currency on the design scene, Adjaye is holding dear a set of true values as he throws in his lot with architectural democracy. ⚙

Above
With a 'dance floor' on its
ground floor, the new Louis
Vuitton store in Tokyo, designed
by Eric Carlson of Louis
Vuitton, Jun Aoki and Aurelio
Clementi, takes its inspiration
from the club scene in the
nearby Roppongi crossing
area of the city. Upstairs, the
clubbing theme continues
with a 'Bag Bar', 'Shoe Salon'
and 'Luggage Lounge'.

Jonathan Bell is a writer and freelance journalist. His books include *Concept Car Design* (RotoVision, 2003) and *Carchitecture* (editor, August 2001). He has contributed to *Wallpaper**, *Blueprint*, *Viewpoint* and *Graphics International* (now *Grafik*), and is also the co-editor of *things*, a journal of writing about objects and their histories. He lives in London.

Helen Castle is editor of *Architectural Design* and executive commissioning editor of Wiley-Academy.

Jonathan Clarke joined the Universal Design Studio in 2002 as a director. He has considerable experience as an architect in practice (with Echo Sounder and Urban Research Lab) and teaching (the Architectural Association, South Bank and Brighton universities, and visiting lecturer at Oxford University and Princeton). Formed in July 2001 by Edward Barber and Jay Osgerby, the studio was a natural development from the success of the high-profile product designs of Barber Osgerby. It is a multidisciplinary design studio specialising in architectural, industrial design and interior projects, and is responsible for designing Stella McCartney's flagship stores in London and New York, and for the redesign of Damien Hirst's Pharmacy.

London-based **Eleanor Curtis** has worked as a writer and photographer for both news and features with UK and international broadsheets, and international journals, for the last nine years. Subjects include architecture, design, urban issues and current news. She is a graduate of the University of Sussex and held a position as research fellow at the Royal College of Art, London, shortly afterwards. She has worked from the Middle East, Italy, Angola and London, and has had two solo photographic exhibitions of her work in Angola. She has published two books with Wiley-Academy: *Hotel Interior Structures* (2001/2003) and *School Builders* (2003).

Lindsay Johnston is a practising architect, teacher and writer. He has designed sports clubs, recreational buildings and stadium facilities in Ireland and the Middle East, and his innovative, environmentally responsive residential designs in Australia have been awarded and published internationally.

Jeremy Melvin is a writer who specialises in architecture. He is a contributing editor to *Architectural Design* and has contributed to many professional, national and international publications. He studied architecture and history of architecture at the Bartlett, UCL, and teaches history of architecture at South Bank University, London, as well as being a consultant to the Royal Academy's architecture programme.

David Sokol is a New York-based writer and managing editor of *ID* magazine. He was most recently associate editor of *Retail Traffic* magazine, and a frequent contributor to *Architectural Record*, *Metropolis* and *Oculus*. He has also written for *Architecture*, *ArcCA* and *The Advocate*, as well as for academic journals.

Masaaki Takahashi is a freelance journalist, covering media, design, pop culture and social issues from an architectural perspective. He writes for various media, and describes his style as 'on-the-street and informative'. He was educated in Tokyo, Berlin, London and New York.

A Floor-to-Ceiling Revolution

Opposite and below left
The elevator lobby of a Miami office building features architect Laurinda Spear's Linework range of textured vinyl wall coverings for Wolf-Gordon, a US supplier.

Below right
The verticality of lobby walls in the office building is enhanced by the modified stripes of the pattern shown here in a colour named 'vence blue'.

Pattern above
Marybeth Shaw hopes Flexuous, a field pattern by industrial designer Karim Rashid, will find a mass audience through her company's commercial clients.

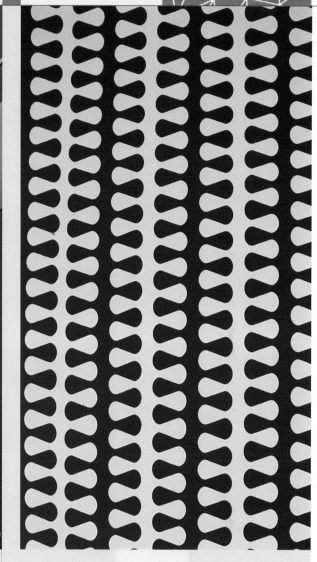

Craig Kellogg describes how, in an industry dominated by neutral wall treatments, a trained architect is leading a splashy wallpaper revival at Wolf-Gordon, and along the way commissioning designs from the likes of Miami architect Laurinda Spear and industrial designer Karim Rashid.

People – especially architects – delight in hating wallpaper. When renovating an old building they rip it down, and for new construction they are loath to install it in the first place. As things now stand, nearly everyone lives and works in painted rooms. This wasn't always the case, however. As few people seem to remember, Le Corbusier created several collections of geometric wallpaper designs in his day. Surprise! The patterned wall coverings from the Bauhaus were bestsellers.

You really have to think back a few decades to find fabulous new wallpapers readily available in the US. As late as the 1960s they were an affordable luxury that conferred a certain kind of respectability on a home. Though wall coverings were expensive to buy and install, people felt they

needed them. And for adventurous middle-class decorators the parade of ever-newer patterns offered instant access to avant-garde designs.

But as papered rooms slipped from fashion, manufacturers became increasingly conservative in their offerings. The range of patterns narrowed, and weak pastels or soft textures supplanted boldly coloured modern designs. The bland new papers – printed on vinyl, actually – were ideal mainly for hotel corridors and care homes for the elderly. Generally, however, architects would specify them only in hospitality situations – limited to areas that demanded extreme durability and fire resistance.

Below left
Laurinda Spear's versatile top seller, Bamboo, in a colour named 'rainforest', served
as the backdrop for the staged promotional photograph of a work station.

Below right and opposite
Karim Rashid's Replicant pattern in magenta dramatically transformed the minimalist
architecture of his own living room, which is a showcase for the furniture he designs.

Pattern above
Marybeth Shaw greatly enlarged the loosely woven
wool threads designer Petra Blaisse supplied
for a pattern called Cord #2. Other photorealistic
patterns in the range imply soft fur or felt.

At the beginning of 2001, the Miami architect Laurinda Spear debuted a collection of crisp, modern vinyls with Wolf-Gordon, a major supplier of commercial wall coverings based in New York. The range was anything but bland. In contrast to the company's popular faux rice-paper or simulated stucco textures, Spear's new patterns were suave pop abstractions. The motifs were based on architectural symbols she adapted from AutoCAD drawings, and though they were cleverly transformed with both scale and colour, they were honest and as easy to read as the purest Modernism. 'It was vinyl wall covering with a print on it, not trying to look like something else,' says Marybeth Shaw, Wolf-Gordon's creative director.

Unlike many in the world of wall coverings, Shaw has a masters degree in city planning from MIT, and another one from L'Ecole d'Architecture de Paris-Belleville in architecture. As she likes to say, good design is about 'dignity and improving the condition of how people live. Otherwise,' she adds, 'why would I waste my time with vinyl wall coverings?'

Designers present their patterns to Shaw as small drawings in black-and-white. The colours are decided later. Not every pattern readily translates into a commercial wall covering, but successful patterns break down into rough categories. There are large-scale stripes or all-over textures. Scatter prints must be large enough in scale to avoid being seen as textures. Strong horizontals, which need to be matched during installation, are discouraged.

Shaw decided to render Spear's patterns with saturated blues, reds and jewel tones that required lots of ink. At the mill she found herself saying 'More, more, more, more, more,' because the colours in the first strike-offs were too 'translucent'. The most exciting opportunity in the printing process is that colours may be substituted freely once the patterns are engraved on to rollers. For example, a bespoke pink-and-purple version of Spear's Wave pattern was used for a care home for the elderly. The architectural

Pattern above
Blaisse supplied a small, crudely
knitted sample that was photographed
and pieced into the repeating pattern
Knitte #1.

justification, according to the project's independent interior designer, was that residents would be less likely to bump into walls and injure themselves.

Based partly on Spear's reputation among architects, the patterns sneaked out of the hospitality ghetto. People wanted them for hotels and restaurants, of course, but also for offices and homes. Suddenly Wolf-Gordon salespeople were welcome at exclusive design firms they previously had no access to. Although hiring Spear was an experiment, it proved a sound business decision when it netted designers who 'wouldn't normally use wallpaper'. Flush with success, Shaw asked the industrial designer Karim Rashid to interpret natural themes digitally on his computer. Rashid proposed tessellated topographies, 3-D geometrics and spaghetti stripes. Though the fluorescent inks he wanted weren't technically possible, lime green and Barbie pink were.

For every geometric, considering colour, scale and the relationship of object to background, there is a threshold where the abstractions begin to have some narrative content. Rashid's patterns exist on the cusp of narrative. People say his Rosetta paper reminds them of goldfish or flower buds. It's said that Replicant, his giant stripe, looks like a femur. But the heroic scale also gives the pattern its architectural presence in, say, a ballroom. 'A microscopic pattern in a large space,' Shaw says, 'is just going to look like paint.'

The company's newest collection is by Petra Blaisse, a Dutch designer known in architectural circles because of her association with Rem Koolhaas. Her trompe l'oeil patterns include wool threads as fat as caterpillars and photorealistic felt and fur. The startling realism of the patterns, Shaw says, gives them power as architectural tools. Perception and, ultimately, architectural space are tweaked by the illusion of a soft, spongy wall plane with space behind it. In breaking walls down visually, Blaisse has quietly moved wall coverings into the realm of phenomenology. Can mind-blowing patterns from Steven Holl or Zaha Hadid be far behind? ᴐ

Below
Each form, such as the void of the swimming pool or the prismatic volume of the gym, is articulated as a coherent series of spaces. Both reuse existing structures but between them, at first-floor level in the gym and slightly overhanging the pool, having an enigmatic relationship to both, is the aluminium-clad aerobics studio.

Educare Sports Facilities, Guadalajara, Mexico

Below right, top
General ground-floor plan. Norten's aim was to orchestrate a dramatic and
varied series of effects within essentially normative forms, but with a variety
of texture, material and lighting effects. The position of the structures and
their construction also modifies the harsh climate to make it as comfortable
as possible for physical exertion.

Bottom
The banded effect of the gym and the lattice grid of
the long 'bar' establish a contrast between what
might otherwise appear to be bland volumes. Both
reveal tantalisingly little about what goes on inside.

Jeremy Melvin describes how for
Enrique Norten of Ten Arquitectos, the
design of a high-school sports facility
presented multiple possibilities and
'undefined opportunities'. Using the
existing foundations as a departure
point, he created rich interstitial spaces
and a performative breathing skin.

Below
Whatever the proscriptions on form at ground level, as it ascends to the roof the gym increasingly
transcends them. Carefully shaping the ceiling soffit and placing a band of translucent glass
panels around the top of the walls gives the ceiling the effect of a plane floating above the floor
level where physical human prowess is put to the test. Below the translucent glass are the louvred
panels that open or close according to climatic and environmental conditions.

If Modernism is genuinely a critical practice, then one measure
of its success lies in the way it interacts with other traditions.
Enrique Norten's firm Ten Arquitectos addresses some of the
rawest interactions imaginable – between divergent economic
circumstances, different construction practices, the dynamic of
tradition and change inherent in large cities – but refracting
them through a Modernist sensibility casts them in a reflective
and dialogic relationship to each other. Though his practice is
split between New York and Mexico City, it is the latter of the
two, where he was born and studied until doing a masters at
Cornell in the US, that 'has informed my work more than any
other experience'. In this formulation, Modernism becomes
a practice that enters into critical engagement with local,
existing and contingent conditions; without rejecting them it
assumes a mutually transformative character. 'Architecture,'
he explains, 'becomes very important.'

The Educare Sports Facilities for a high school in Zapopan,
on the fringe of Mexico's second city Guadalajara,
demonstrates the way he filters traditions of construction and
use into 'particular and specific interventions' in both literal

and symbolic terms. By reusing the foundations of
an old adobe warehouse and cistern it physically and
directly engages with a building tradition that is at
least as old as European settlement in Mexico, and
these foundations set the position and, to some extent,
the shape of the new structures.

But these structures have to relate to a programme,
which here demands accommodation for sports – a
swimming pool, gym with separate spaces for aerobic
and anaerobic exercise, changing rooms and showers
– and functional planning is a fundamental element
of Modernism. Each of these activities has quite
specifically defined spatial requirements, but overlain
on these demands was the additional need for the gym
to be a multipurpose space that could be easily adapted
for various ceremonies and celebrations.

As Norten explained in a lecture at the Royal
Academy in March 2003: 'Fact determines these forms.'
The swimming pool logically reuses the void of the old
cistern; the gym is housed in a new, essentially cuboid

Below
In addition to providing night-time lighting,
the glowing effect picks out the detail and
construction in a quite different manner.

structure at right angles to the pool, and various outdoor
pitches slot in comfortably around them. But pure form is not
what interests Norten: 'There are so many more possibilities.'
What happens around the bland formal 'facts' assumes great
importance; each area interacts, according to its function and
position, with the fluctuating climate and lighting to create a
coherent series of spaces and fields for experiences, and the
effects of their interaction rise above mere contingent fact
or the limitation of any single tradition which they represent.
One of the characteristics of megacities that interests Norten
are the 'undefined opportunities' that inevitably arise in the
intersections between their districts and activities.

A suburban high school is not a megacity, but the given
accidents of form represented by the existing foundations
might stand as an analogue of the districts of one, and the
manner in which Norten has articulated the interstices
between the 'formal facts' indicates something of the way
he might address a complex urban site.

At Educare the obvious need to protect the outdoor pool from
a harsh and dusty northerly wind becomes a cue to play with the
variable effects of walls and enclosures. Belying its
origins in the accidental form of a cistern, wrapping the
pool on three sides by a stone wall clearly articulates it as
an outdoor room, while the fourth side is a long 'bar' with
changing and exercise rooms, clad in concrete on the pool
side, though an outdoor ramp leading to the first floor
makes it less inscrutable. On the opposite side of the 'bar'
building is a lattice of glass blocks, which at night glows
with light to illuminate the soccer pitch. A wall is not just
a wall, nor an enclosure a simple definition of space, but
an opportunity to orchestrate a series of effects which
vary according to conditions, use and the time of day.

Using static walls to form intimate enclosures that
modulate the climatic extremes is only part of the
strategy. When designing the gym itself Norten posed
the question: 'How does nature do it?' Among other
means is the way fish scales automatically close to
keep the animal at an even temperature when that of
the water fluctuates. Translating organic metaphors
into architecture can be literal or laboured, but for Norten

Top
First-floor plan. The aerobics studio hovers above the
walkway between the pool and the gym. Though not
attached to either, it has a tenuous connection to both.

Bottom
Ground-floor plan. As well as providing sports
facilities, the gym has to be flexible enough to
be usable for various school ceremonies as well.

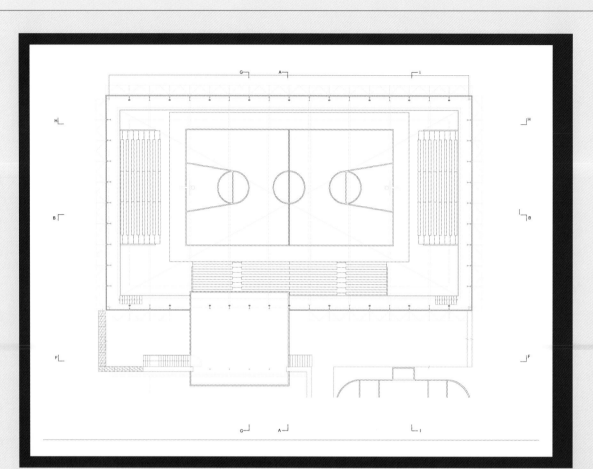

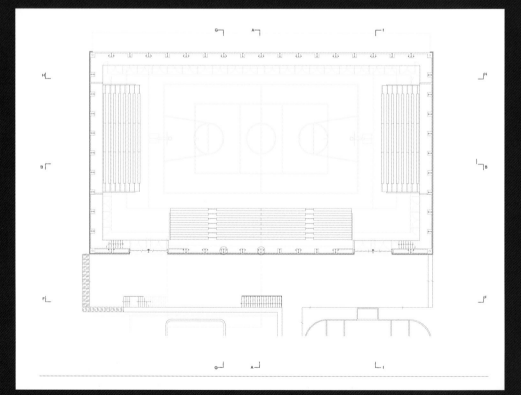

Top left and right
West facade (left) and Section B-B (right). The facades are clearly
banded to deal with specific functions; the lowest level defines the
space for sport, the intermediate strip modifies the climate while
the upper band modulates the light. Inside, these three bands
interact with human activities, participating or spectating.

Middle left and right
Section G-G (left), showing the aerobics box in relation to the gym. Sectional
elevation (right) from the swimming pool showing the aerobics box.

Bottom left and right
South (left) and north (right) facades. Using natural sunlight and allowing the
building to breathe through opening louvres results in a significant energy saving.

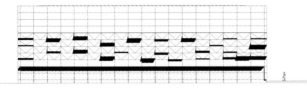

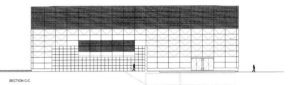

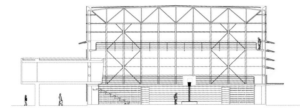

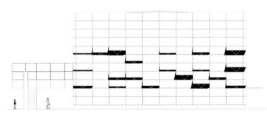

SECTION C-C

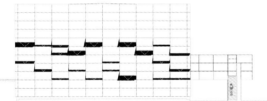

it was a way of giving the skin of an otherwise simple prismatic
form some life. Movable louvres clad the building's lower two-
thirds, opening and closing at different times according to
climatic conditions. Treating the skin of a building as if it were a
breathing membrane is a common theme in Ten's projects and is
again a way of transforming a practical device into poetic effect.
It can act as a buffer zone to minimise temperature fluctuations
inside, but in establishing layers of acoustic and visual privacy
it also helps to define perceptions of the design. In some cases,
too, these interstitial spaces transform the way individual
buildings adapt themselves to a climatic or urban environment,
becoming metaphors for the urban condition of large cities.

The visual effects of the breathing membrane at the Educare
gym are extraordinary. In a gym, functional requirements are
fairly prescriptive: a wood floor with markings for various
sports, a high ceiling and generally seating, in this case on one
long and two short sides. But few gyms have a roof that seems
to hover above the playing area, an illusion created by sloping it
upwards towards the edges, which accordingly catch light from
the ring of high-level frosted-glass panels. Together these filter
and control sunlight, so it is uniform enough for sport (the

filters take out the fluctuations in light level when the
sun goes in and comes out, which can be very disturbing
during ball games in particular). If the building's
enclosure has an obvious purpose of creating
appropriate conditions for various sporting activities
from those that naturally prevail in the area, it also
has a secondary effect running in the opposite direction:
to suggest to those participating in the humanly
ordained activities of sport, whose outcome depends
on physical prowess, that there might also be a
metaphysical aspect to their existence.

A glass and aluminium volume, used for aerobics,
projects from the gym at first-floor level over the
swimming pool, bringing a vestige of the theme of
hovering to the outside. But it is at night that the various
conditions of solid and void, light and shade, transparency
and translucency, merge. Just as the glass-block wall
on the 'bar' illuminates the soccer pitch, so the gym
glows like a giant lamp, its light reflected in the pool.
Here the numerous strands of tradition and purpose
dissolve into a series of ethereal effects. ⚏

107+

Freecell Freecell

'OPEN: New Designs for Public Space', Van Alen Institute
For the summer 2003 exhibit 'OPEN: New Designs for Public Space', Freecell transformed the wooden floors and white walls of the Van Alen Institute into the 'emersive space' and 'coolest lobby you'd ever walk into' that the clients requested. Aqua paint covers walls, ceiling and the underside of Plexiglass panels screwed to the floor, which in the hot summer weather rippled, reflecting light and images in

Freecell

Over the summer a young Brooklyn-based practice wowed the Manhattan architecture community with a workshop-crafted installation at the Van Alen Institute, New York. **Karen A Franck** explains how Freecell draws its inspiration from the everyday industrial and commercial landscape of New York and New Jersey, transforming 'what is functional and necessary' into 'something beautiful to behold and to use'.

Freecell Freecell

wavy patterns. Designed and built as modules to be transported to the exhibit's next venue, the steel frame of the exhibit structure of bents and runners attaches to studs in the wall, projecting outwards 16 inches and 'removing the images from the spatial envelope' of the room, according to the architects, and hiding 10 TV monitors that show videos of completed projects. Mounted exhibit images slide and lock into aluminium channels, allowing for changes and alternative arrangements, while text panels remain fixed. The firm Flat designed the graphics for the show. Movable modular seating, also covered in aqua Plexiglass with the same exposed steel framing of the exhibit structure, allows for lounging and perching. Bold aqua graphics on the window proclaim the exhibit's title to the street below.

Exiting the elevator, I enter a sea of blue: blue is everywhere, even shimmering underfoot. This must be the wrong floor. As I turn away, I catch sight of familiar faces. So this is the Van Alen Institute? Yes, but transformed into a cool aqua swimming pool for the summer 2003 exhibit 'OPEN: New Designs for Public Space'. Asked by Van Alen director Ray Gastil and exhibit curator Zoé Ryan to create a total environment that would make visitors feel 'they were in a different world', this is exactly what Freecell did. Rejecting their own initial idea of building structures for visitors to climb into, the architects suggested that the entire gallery space could become the new environment and, because 'they could see how transformative simple things are', according to Ryan, Freecell accomplished this with paint and Plexiglass – in all the right places.

In their own shop at their studio in the Dumbo neighbourhood of Brooklyn, Freecell builds the installations they design, delivering them in modules for assembly at the site. This combination of design and fabrication allows the team to be both 'ambitious and realistic', says Ryan. Very quickly they can estimate what is feasible and affordable and what is not; they do not have to depend on others to meet budgets and schedules; and they can ensure that the clarity and quality promised in their designs are met in the completed work.

Equally important, Freecell's use of relatively inexpensive materials allows clients to pay for innovative design and meticulous fabrication, and not for high-end materials. Bill Bergeron of New York video-graphics design firm Verb Media remarked: 'When you do something that has high precision but low material value, it rubs against a traditional mode of construction,' adding that 'most art is built this way.' Freecell 'will take on more and do more than other architects often do because they build it themselves,' he continues.

Verb Media

A sensuous counter/storage unit snakes through the airy loft space of Verb Media, separating a visitors' waiting area from the production area. This curving sculpture of plywood and fibreboard accommodates, with great specificity, the multitude of objects and tasks associated with the business of designing graphics for TV and film. Where the visitor enters, a pull-out computer and file drawers aid the receptionist/accountant; further along, other shelves and cabinets store books and tools of the trade while pull-out shelves allow easy but hidden access to printers and fax machines. At a break in the counter there is room to do paste-up work. On the production side, the structure changes shape to make space for a coffee machine, water cooler, refrigerator, rubbish bin, microwave – an entire kitchenette – and a video monitor.

Freecell seems to relish the challenges their design ideas and the clients' constraints pose. To ensure affordability and elegance they make ingenious use of common materials and off-the-shelf items. At Verb Media, curtains screening the conference room and editing bay now hang from tracks usually used in hospital rooms, while curtains on the windows are made from plastic-coated agricultural screening commonly used to cover greenhouses. Steel conduit tubing made to support awnings came in handy to build the shelving/seating structure for the Shortwave Bookstore and to frame the kitchenette unit for the Sarah Meltzer Gallery.

The three founding partners met at architecture school. John Hartmann and Lauren Crahan went to the Rhode Island School of Design; Lauren graduated while John moved on to The Cooper Union where he met Troy Ostrander, who had already received a bachelor of science in architecture from the University of Michigan. John and Troy completed their first project, a new office for Liquid Design, before they graduated from Cooper. Associate Corey Yurkovich came to Freecell from Kent State University, also with a bachelor of architecture degree. A true collaborative team, their individual strengths differ: Troy directs the shop and determines what is feasible and how; Lauren takes on code issues, construction documents and communication with other professionals; John's strong point is computer rendering and other forms of visualisation; and Corey brings welding and graphic-design skills to the team.

Hartmann reports that the group's most creative and productive time is when they all sit down together at a

At the far end, the counter grows again, becoming wheeled
carts for video storage. Quilted curtains can be drawn around
the conference area and the editing bay. Visiting clients have
said it is the nicest office they've ever seen.

large table and do a series of individual drawings to generate
initial ideas for a project. He emphasises that they 'never mix
ideas; that would compromise the simplicity'. After several
sketches they reach consensus about which idea will work
best, and then all of them work, separately, to develop that one
idea. John remembers that the Shortwave Bookstore solution
was Troy's idea: 'I tried and tried to outthink him but I couldn't.
You have to come to that realisation – that you have to let the
better idea win out.'

Freecell draws inspiration from the everyday industrial and
commercial landscapes of New York and New Jersey – some
derelict, many still in use. In public lectures, as they refer to their
mission of 'finding architecture' and 'finding form', a sequence of
striking images of such places appears on screen without a
single view of what is commonly called 'architecture'. Recurring

themes in these images – strong colours, repetition,
proliferation of containers, exposure of structure and craft
of making – appear in Freecell's work. As in Freecell's
images of industrial landscapes, the quotidian is given
pride of place: what is functional and necessary is treated
with respect, even love, becoming something beautiful
to behold and to use. 'Form is found' in the everyday
tasks and needs of clients. Key to these needs in today's
world is storage, which Freecell treats as a wellspring
for design. One imagines that the architects' first question
to a client might be 'Let's see your stuff'.

Partners Bill Bergeron and Greg Duncan at Verb
Media took digital photographs and made lists of all
the materials and equipment they depend on in their
video-graphics design business and then asked for

Art in General

Freecell's proposal for Art in General is one of five winning schemes in the competition for the redesign of the gallery's two floors on Walker Street. Displayed in the current gallery in spring 2003, in drawings and a built portion of the project that one could occupy, the design was notable for its combination of simplicity and richness. A series of two smaller galleries on the lower floor and a larger, taller main gallery on the upper floor are pristine white boxes. Wrapping the galleries is continuous floor-to-ceiling plywood shelving for the storage of books, boxes and art materials accessible to the offices, library and classroom adjacent to the galleries. As visitors proceed through the sequence of galleries, including one in the stairwell linking the fourth and sixth floors, they glimpse the shelving and the work spaces that serve and support them. Immediately upon arrival, the visitor sees 'both elements – the offices as the complicated and busy office side and the gallery as the serene reflective side'.

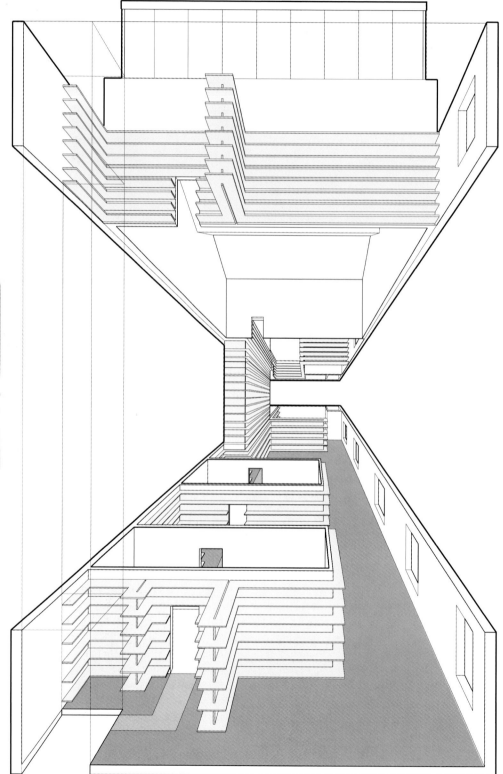

triple the amount of storage space they were using. While 'early schemes were interesting conceptually, they did not hold up to the functionality required', says Bergeron. In the end, the counter/storage that winds through the office not only creates a variety of spaces of different shapes but also houses a place, suitably sized and appropriately accessible, for almost every item in the office. When the item is large, the place for it becomes a visually significant form in the continuous 'band' of storage. Freecell's attention to the size and shape of each item is also evident in their adaptation of an airstream trailer for the Bookmobile mobile exhibition space: the team measured each book in the display to ensure that every size was accommodated.

Storage is joined with display and seating in the units Freecell invented for the 'Future Furniture' exhibit at the Chicago Design Show in 2000. Thickly painted wooden stools with lacquered-steel feet become covers for compartmentalised wall shelving; the feet of these stools are inserted into a grid of holes in the shelving. And at the Shortwave Bookstore, storage is again combined with display and seating in a tall, curved structure that holds books for sale and boxes of books in overstock on the convex side, and becomes seating on the concave side.

This pairing of storage with display and the double-sidedness of a structure reappear in Freecell's proposal for the redesign of the Art in General gallery. What is plywood shelving for the work spaces on one side becomes the pristine walls of the galleries on the other. And, significantly, both shelving and work spaces are visible to visitors as they move from one gallery space to the next: the quotidian must get its due, its place in the sun. At the same time, a point is simply

and eloquently made: the administration supports the gallery and the gallery supports the administration.

That Freecell designs and builds furniture, such as the storage/seating and a 'tractor chair', independently of their interior architecture projects reflects their interest in the body, at rest and moving, and its experience of space. For the tractor chair, the firm attached a modified tractor/combine seat of bright-yellow vinyl to a base of bent tubing. To exhibit Le Corbusier's section drawings of his Baghdad stadium at the Henry Urbach Architecture gallery, Freecell placed each drawing between two glass panels and hung the series of 10 from the ceiling, allowing visitors to walk around them and to see through the openings Corbusier had made in them. Sections through the right side of the stadium hung in a row on the right side of the room, facing the front, while sections through the left side of the stadium hung on the left, facing the back of the gallery. The strong diagonal line of the stadium seating always descended from upper right to lower left, down to the aisle between the two rows – to the floor of the stadium. This arrangement drew the visitor down one row and up the other. The path through the Art in General project is a spatially and visually rich procession even though the design concept is simple and direct. Staff at the Shortwave Bookstore climb directly on the structure or lean and hang on to it when they use a ladder. Summer intern Ana Saldamando reports: 'It feels a little precarious

Shortwave Bookstore
When Shortwave, the book shop of Soft Skull Press, moved to a Brooklyn store-front from the entry area of a club on the Lower East Side in 2002, they could bring their signature shelving/seating structure with them. The convex side of this floor-to-ceiling, curved, ladder-like frame displays books for sale and provides storage space for overstock, while the concave side offers seating that is intimate without being dark. Built in modules and made of bent-steel conduit tubing, commonly used for awning support, the frame is sturdy enough to climb on, something staff often do to rearrange displays and reach the overstock. Visually striking and a highly efficient use of space, staff also report the frame is fun to climb on. Publisher Richard Nash marvels that it has volume without mass, noting that it is popular with the media, who enjoy incorporating it into photographs

of store events. In Brooklyn the frame attaches to a wall of double-sided, plywood shelving that displays more books for sale on the store side (in the 'cave') and provides storage for the publishing company's office space on the other.

Below right
Kitchenette, Sarah Meltzer Gallery, New York.

but that's the fun of it. We're definitely a young place – that's our energy – and this is right for us.'

While the Art in General proposal outlines a truly rebuilt environment (walls and a raised roof), Freecell frequently creates environments with no, or just minor, interventions in the existing structure. A dim hallway at the Jacobs Javits Convention Center became a landscape of hilly mounds of wheat grass, which Freecell germinated from seed, for the International Contemporary Furniture Fair. This talent, so apparent in the Henry Urbach and Van Alen exhibits, was one reason why Freecell received the Van Alen commission. Movement, rest and environment are joined together in Freecell's installation 'Beneath', exhibited at Artists Space in New York and Rhode Island School of Design. A somewhat mysterious series of connected volumes raised off the floor on a structural system encourages movement from one module to another as well as sitting, perching and lying down, all of which visitors do without instruction.

Freecell has not yet completed a building but in 2004 they expect construction to begin on a house they have designed for a site on the Palm Coast in Florida. This time Freecell are the designers but not the builders. Excited about the prospect of designing more complex structural and mechanical systems, the group already finds it 'a little hard to let go'. However, as Lauren Crahan explains, if they find contractors who are as excited and committed as they are, those people 'can become part of the team and "freecell" will have much more meaning – because it's not about individuals, it's about all of us coming together to make the project.'

Karen A Franck is a professor at the New Jersey School of Architecture and the Department of Social Sciences and Humanities at the New Jersey Institute of Technology. She has contributed to Δ before, most recently two articles in *Food and Architecture* (2002), which she guest-edited. Always interested in how design can support and enhance daily life, she focused on that topic in her book *Architecture Inside Out* (Wiley-Academy, 2000), written with Bianca Lepori. Karen has a PhD in environmental psychology from the City University of New York.

Below left and right
Storage/seating unit.

Below
Freecell, from left to right:
John Hartmann, Lauren Crahan,
Troy Ostrander and Corey Yurkovich.

FreecellResumé

1997	Liquid Design, new offices, New York
1999	Artisan, new offices, New York
	Horodniceau Apartment, New York
2000	Shortwave Bookstore 1, New York
	Storage/seating unit
2001	Bookmobile, mobile exhibition space, US and Canada
	Tractor chair
2002	Shortwave Bookstore 2, Brooklyn
	Grasscape International Contemporary Furniture Fair, New York

Kitchenette, Sarah Meltzer Gallery, New York
'Beneath', Artists Space, New York
Miller Projection Screen, New York

2003   'OPEN' exhibit, Van Alen Institute, New York

Verb Media, new video-graphics design offices, New York
Art in General gallery proposal, New York
Far and Near exhibit, Henry Urbach Architecture gallery, New York
Peckolick/Drexler Apartment, New York
Graham Residence, Palm Coast, Florida (construction 2004)

Walt Disney Concert Hall, Los Angeles, California
Architect: Gehry Partners Engineer: John A Martin & Associates
The architect's conceptual sketch of a complex form which cannot
be realised using implicitly understood, conventional construction
techniques, initiates an extensive process of digitally aided
research and refinement.

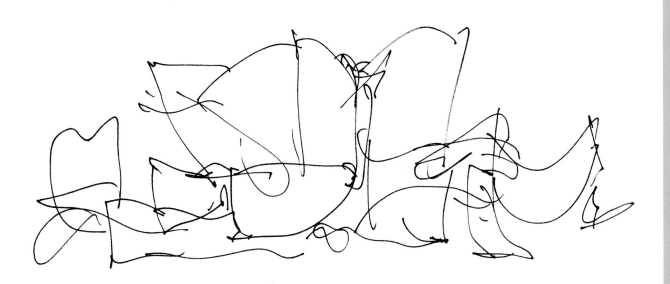

CAD/CAM in the Business of Architecture, Engineering and Construction

Digital tools offer us powerful new means of generating, describing,
analysing, refining and constructing architectural projects, as we
have seen in previous articles of the 'Blurring the Lines' series.
This final article sheds some light on the professional practice
impacts of CAD/CAM adoption, relating a recent conversation of
André Chaszar with **James Glymph** of Gehry Partners about the
organisational, contractual and legal issues facing designers and
builders who wish to better integrate their work. It reveals that
although the technical challenges to be overcome in applying CAD/CAM
to architecture are formidable, they are frequently trumped by the
obstacles potentially posed by entrenched procedural constraints.

117+

Walt Disney Concert Hall, Los Angeles, California
Below
Digital 3-D modelling of the building's architectural, structural and environmental
systems shows an advanced state of coordination among design disciplines
and building trades which also enables negotiation of conflicting requirements.

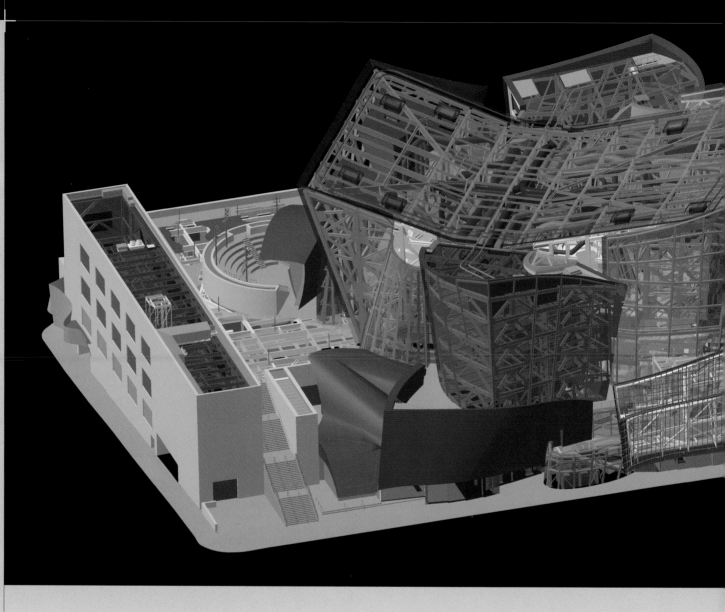

The advanced descriptive, analytical and communicative capabilities of digital tools are encouraging their ever wider adoption in the building industry, which is now beginning to come to grips with the practicalities of leveraging the computing power that has revolutionised the industrial design, electronics, aircraft, boat-building and auto industries. A significant number of architects have been encouraged by these technologies to propose and undertake projects of much greater complexity (whether formal, organisational or both) than are found in conventional contemporary practice, and the engineers and builders with whom they work are correspondingly challenged to bring CAD/CAM to bear in their own work. But it is precisely this concept of 'their own' work that poses the largest questions, the greatest challenges: in blurring the lines between architecture, engineering and building, what becomes of the lines of ownership and responsibility?

Decades, even centuries, of effort have gone into creating the present sets of regulations and contractual forms governing the design and construction of buildings. Older still are the concepts of property that are an underlying motivation of much human activity. Digital working, on the other hand, implies (if it does not demand) a significant transgression of many of these boundaries. Certainly a good number of the most significant digitally produced buildings have, in one or more respects, succeeded by bridging over these barriers, allowing these projects to make the most of interdisciplinary collaboration and in many cases the elision of normally distinct building functions. Should all digitally produced works strive to do the same? What can architects, engineers, builders, building owners (perhaps even regulators and attorneys) do to facilitate such blurring where it is deemed desirable?

Below right, top
Digital modelling of the structure serves for visualisation, coordination and structural analysis, facilitating collaboration but also requiring verification by the different parties using it for different purposes.

Below bottom
Mixed-media design exploration utilises physical study models digitised for further analysis. At later stages in the project, laser scanning of the as-built structure plays a role in fitting the cladding system to compensate for erection tolerances.

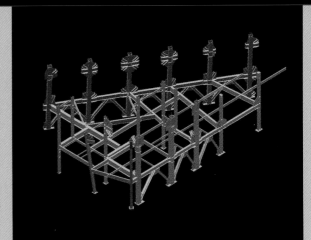

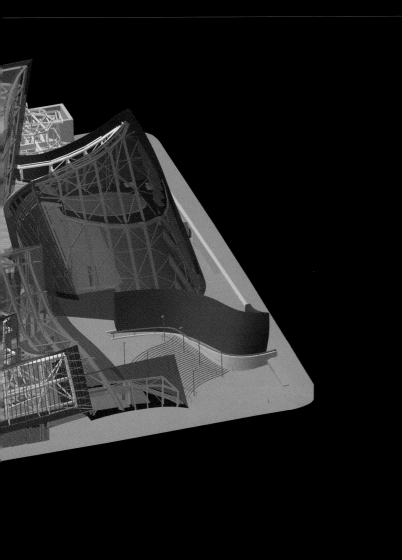

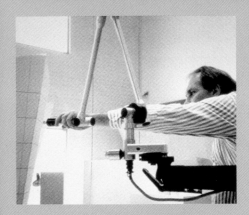

To be sure, questions like these are not entirely unique to the building industry. Ever widening adoption of the Internet has raised a host of intellectual property issues, and a burgeoning branch of legal effort is emerging to address these. On the other hand, many of the other industries to which the digital evangelical in architecture point as exemplars do not face the same hurdles. Specifically, the aircraft and automotive industries, as well as industrial design producers (of consumer goods, etc) tend to encompass the entire conception and production in-house, with only limited outsourcing. Design-build, if you will. Boat-builders differ somewhat, more nearly approaching the fragmented supply chain typical of building construction as noted earlier, and they are therefore perhaps a more relevant example to architecture, though their logistical challenges are still not as extensive. Yet the problems in building persist. The architects develop a digital model which their various engineering and other consultants can readily analyse and, where necessary, reconfigure. Assuming that after all of the modifications are made someone can check that the design 'documents' (are they drawings, models, digital, physical?) are correct: Who owns the design? Say that constructibility and other logistical and economic factors are successfully addressed through early involvement of the contractors: Who is responsible for 'means and methods'?

Rethinking the procurement process required to fully exploit CAD/CAM's advantages leads generally to design-build as the preferred paradigm, in which many of the customary defensive obstacles are mitigated or eliminated by sharing financial risk and reward. Whereas the conventional 'throw it over the fence' organisational model does at least have the advantage of giving fairly hard and fast rules about responsibility and the compensation for accepting it, the seamless flow envisioned by digital working methods requires

MIT **Stata Center**
Architect: Gehry Partners Engineer: John A Martin & Associates
Construction document drawing illustrating different elements of the 3-D
database: geometry, site work, cladding pattern, MEP, framing and structure.

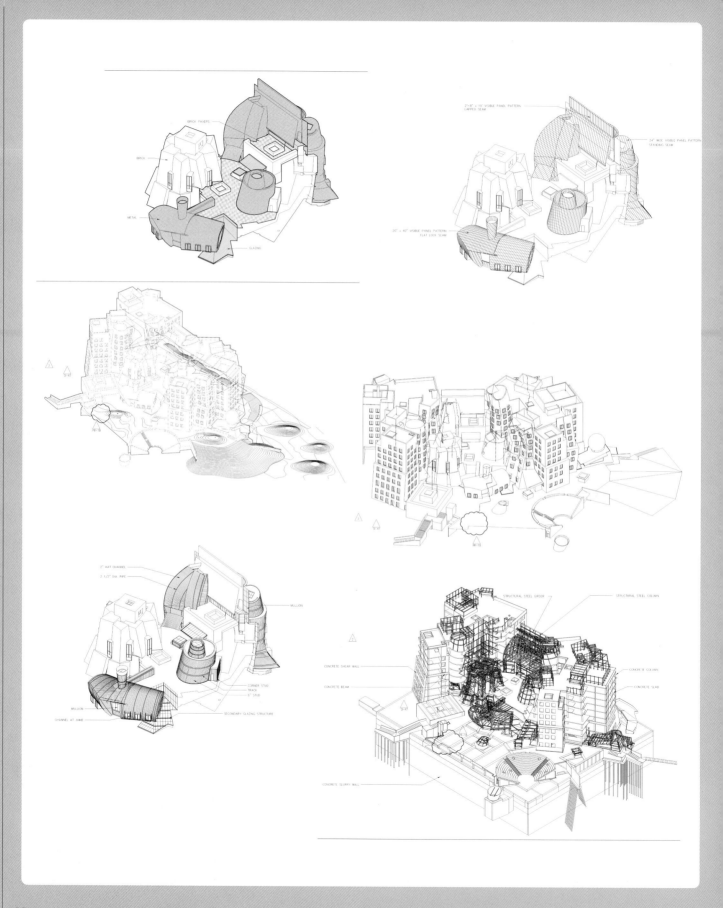

Zollhof apartments, Düsseldorf, Germany
Architect: Gehry Partners Contractor: Philipp Holzmann AG
Below left and right
A study model rough-out digitally and finished manually describes volumes to be constructed
in precast concrete. The shape of the panels challenges conventional forming and reinforcing
practices, requiring close collaboration between designers and contractors.

much greater flexibility (and perhaps agility) from the participants. James Glymph says that the success of a collaboration among architects, engineers and builders depends to a great extent simply on their willingness to 'throw away the rule book' and streamline the flow of information and ideas where they see mutual advantage in doing so. Often, if the majority of the project team proposes to work this way, the building owner will go along with this.

As an alternative, Glymph reminds us that recent studies in the US have indicated that negotiated-bid (or 'CM at risk') contracts result in only slightly greater cost and time but much greater client satisfaction than does design-build. In order to effect this, architects can in some cases work from the outset of a project (or special part of a project) with contractors able to use CAD/CAM effectively, negotiating a price and allowing the design to evolve longer into the construction documentation phase. In so doing they may eliminate conventional documentation and its attendant production costs, duplication of effort and inaccuracies in large measure.

Within a more conventional procurement scheme, architects can prequalify contractors with CAD/CAM capability, recognising that they must also accommodate conventionally skilled ones for particular aspects of the project. Success on this front depends largely on the designers' abilities to either produce fabrication information that the contractors can use with confidence or find contractors who have already converted to digital production. Frequently the result is not a less expensive project but an equally expensive though more complex one, and the amount of the designers' time required for troubleshooting is substantial.

In any procurement scheme, then, architects and engineers can aim to design mainly in 3-D and derive the required 2-D documents (as needed by building officials, some non-CAM-capable contractors, etc) from 3-D models, in order not to incur a large premium for duplicated effort. This of course requires software with appropriate capabilities 'out of the box' or jury-rigged in-house. The former is less prevalent and the latter more so, leading all but the most committed designers to continue working in 2-D, but the emerging availability of better tools with more seamless modelling-drawing integration and object-oriented data structures means that we can look forward to more widespread adoption of 'whole building' digital models in the coming years, with more promiscuous information-sharing as a result.

What sorts of 'checks and balances' can the project team bring to bear in order to maintain the quality of their work in such fluid circumstances? Some sort of 'master model' in digital format is essential, says Glymph. Typically this model will describe the primary geometric characteristics of the project and, in the case of components that are 'digitally contracted', also the scope of the work as a quantity output from the model. Sometimes the geometric relationships are definable by rules (as in parametric relational modelling) and in this case it may suffice to transmit these rules to each of the project's participants for them to reconstruct their own copies of the model. In the absence of such rules, as with 'point clouds' and other highly complex spatial data, the individual data points themselves must be

Zollhof apartments, Düsseldorf, Germany
Below
CNC milling of foam to create unique forms for concrete casting enables complex shapes while keeping labour costs acceptable. Recyclability of the foam also helps in cost control as well as addressing environmental concerns. Research is required by both designers and contractors to identify a suitable production method.

transmitted to all concerned. In either case it is then the responsibility of each party to verify the accuracy of the model upon which they will build their own components of the project.

Of course, updating the master model and all derivative models will be necessary as the project evolves, and the amount of effort and degree of reliability associated with these updates is a matter of significant concern. Clearly the updating process is easiest when all parties use a common modelling platform (and in some cases consultants' and contractors' participation in the project may be made contingent upon obtaining the requisite software), but this is not always possible. Parametric and similar modelling capability may also be preferable when design changes are definable as incremental rather than wholesale modifications. Let us bear in mind, though, that the entire issue of design change notifications is not well resolved in the building industry generally (visualise the difficulty of spotting individual but not always explicitly specified changes by overlaying physical drawings or layers of digital drawings), so we can expect that digital technologies will perhaps improve upon and not degrade current performance if proper contract standards are developed. In the short term, and for project teams not yet wise in the ways of digital production, it is possible that the rate of increase in complexity (of buildings or just of data structures) outpaces the improvement in the ability to coordinate complexity.

The significance of these advances depends on which participants (in the design, engineering and fabrication process) develop the complete technical model. To get the most from this approach A&E teams need to be more aware of fabrication issues but, as pointed out by Glymph and others, many architects simply do not want the level of involvement (and corresponding control and responsibility) that the CAD/CAM continuum can offer. It is true that architects typically do not have, nor perhaps even want, the skills required to specify means and methods of construction. However, they can synthesise the abilities and coordinate the efforts of contractors, suggest construction systems and design within, or nearly within, the constraints imposed by available means of production supported by accurate (digital) documentation that contractors can rely on. Where successful, this method can result in improved economy as well as more ambitious designs, because much of the contractor's effort expended in interpreting and re-presenting the design becomes unnecessary.

For those architects and engineers who do take on this expanded area of responsibility, careful consideration is necessary of the skills required to produce reliable data for digitally driven manufacturing, lest they end up producing and 'owning' a pile of scrap,

Below
Digitally and manually produced components must be combined even on the most
digitally advanced building-scale projects, either in very close proximity such
as the CNC-milled formwork and hand-bent reinforcing shown here, or in looser
arrangements. Coordinating the work of contractors with differing capabilities
remains as great a task as in conventional construction, if not greater.

as cautioned by Tim Eliassen in his article in this 'Blurring the Lines' series (see 4, vol 73, no 3, May/June 2003 . Currently there are only limited technological means of assuring such quality. Instead, it is a matter of designers acquiring the necessary knowledge through formal or informal education, ranging from early exposure to such issues in their university coursework through opportunities to practise at the entire design/detail/fabricate continuum on the job, and perhaps even to internships or other practical experience in the employment of CAM-capable builders. (This is not a new prescription, by the way, but only a reiteration of a long-standing call for designers to reacquaint themselves with the problems of building in order to be more effective designers, a call now lent additional weight by the integrative potentials of CAD/CAM.)

The outcome of the emerging power of information technology, in Glymph's view, is that architects should leverage their improved design and communication capabilities in order to continue to be able to offer 'architectural design' – that is, inclusion of attention to human factors – at an acceptably low premium. Otherwise building owners may resort exclusively to ordering buildings from design-build firms which will be able to design facilities using parametrised models of building types, for example. Thus, the ultimate questions are not about how to use computers but: Who will take best advantage of them, and what will be the effect on the built environment?

To summarise, existing contract forms require some modification, to encourage information flow among the parties involved in a project and best realise the advantages of CAD/CAM, if the current multiparty model of project-team composition is to survive, such as where architects work with contractors

through a CM at risk. Education of designers requires some modification to better qualify them for working within such procurement processes. Collaboration between architects, engineers, fabricators and contractors must be encouraged, beginning in schools. Sadly, the opposite is often the case today – at both the educational and professional levels. Software (and to some extent hardware) must continue to develop in the direction of more useful functionality (both general and building-oriented), more transparent and reliable data-transfer among applications, and better user interfaces that do not require extensive programming skills in obtaining useful results with reasonable effort.

And as for the revolutionary impact of new materials and fabrication processes, it seems likely these will take care of themselves inasmuch as human inventiveness continues to unearth heretofore unimagined materials and processes and continues to rediscover and reapply old ones. ∆

This article concludes the 2003 volume of 'Engineering Exegesis' in ∆+.
The following volume will present a series of case studies in which projects
realised with CAD/CAM techniques will illustrate the issues raised so far.

James Glymph is a senior partner of Gehry Partners, LLC. His work at Gehry's
office has been recognised as pioneering in the application of advanced computer
technology to building design and construction.

André Chaszar is the editor of the 'Blurring the Lines' article series, a member of the
∆ editorial advisory board and the founder of O-Design Research and Consulting,
a practice specialising in innovative building systems. He continues his research into
CAD/CAM applications to building through his writing and experimental construction
projects, as well as through consulting to architects and teaching technical
seminars. He is also editing a more extensive collection of articles on CAD/CAM for
architecture which is scheduled for publication by Wiley-Academy in summer 2004.

Wayfinder:

Cate Consandine and Nicholas Murray at Conical, April 2003

Leon van Schaik explains how 'simple layers of light, sound, performance and urban history' combined to create a captivating installation at the Conical gallery in Melbourne, Australia.

Conical is a gallery situated in Fitzroy, one of Melbourne's inner-city suburbs. This suburb, to the north of the original city grid that twitches away from the cardinal points to align with the river running southwest stretches from high ground on the magnetically aligned east–west axis of Victoria Street/Avenue, and continues in an orthogonal grid to Alexandra Avenue at the base of a long north-facing slope. Johnston Street divides the suburb in parallel, and is a major route to the eastern suburbs, bisecting Brunswick Street, Fitzroy's main north–south route.

This suburb was both a first and a last for Melbourne: the first suburb beyond the original city grid and the last to embody an 18th-century model of mixed development, with grand terrace houses for the wealthy lining major streets, and mews and workers' cottages in the areas behind, along with a comprehensive mixture of shops, workshops and factories spread throughout. This mix has made it a vital part of the city's cultural life, as artists and dealers have found different niches for their activities at different stages in their careers.

The Conical gallery embodies the heterogeneity of Fitzroy. A 1920s 'streamline' facade sweeps along a three-storey concrete-frame building on Rochester Street, a narrow lane, encompassing an older building on Johnston Street. This older building is two storeys high, with load-bearing brick and roofed in a pyramidal corrugated-iron roof hidden by the parapet from eyes on the street.

I have taken the trouble to sketch in this locational history here because the work that Cate Consandine and Nicholas Murray installed in the gallery in April 2003 is a superb act of curation of some carefully selected aspects of the city within which they work. Firstly they have created a bicameral distinction in the gallery between the old and the new.

The gallery entrance is on Rochester Street, up a concrete staircase on the south side of the building. So it is that you enter the concrete-frame-and-slab-constructed newer half of the gallery at a corner on the long axis. Consandine and Murray have made this first space into a pristine white cuboid, blanking off the windows, painting everything except the polished timber floor, and lighting it with powerful arc lamps facing the entry and located on the concrete beam that forms the opening to the older part of the gallery to north. In this older, unlit space, the walls have been taken back to the brick, and an early eau-de-nil paint scheme is revealed. Six immaculate joinery replicas of windows finished in satin-sheen white cover the existing windows and suggest a window where the rhythm leads you to expect one. Above, the ceiling has been removed and an aluminium-lined pyramid space is faintly discernible above the timber trusses.

The first thing visitors to the gallery become aware of is this history of development, from the 'organic' brickwork of the 19th century to the aseptic surface-

Opposite
Period gallery space.

Below left
Window panel detail.

Below, top
Transition detail.

Below, bottom
White gallery space.

whiteness of the 20th century. Next they begin to focus on the larger urban grid outside, and on every traffic-light policed intersection in that grid, at which there are push-button-controlled acoustic pedestrian signals that click slowly while the crossing lights are red, and accelerate peremptorily when they turn green.

Murray has recorded hundreds of these sounds, made by 'clackers', none of which operate at quite the same speed, and has composed them into a sequence that is relayed through dozens of hidden speakers in the roof space of the gallery where these rhythmic clicking passages cross over above your head in twisting cascades of lulling patience and then impatient urgency. Your attention drifts from side to side of the darkened second space, and every now and again you lose track of any sense that there is sound at all. So it is that the enhanced facture of the room competes for the visitor's attention with the compelling swelling of the sound, so familiar and yet so displaced from street to room.

This double curation is accompanied by a third, which acts through the personages of the Fitzroy city scene. When you enter the space intent on seeing who else is there, you see only the stark white of the first space, before the faint clicking of the clackers summons you across the super-lit space. You freeze, aware that you are captured in the gaze of people unknown. As you walk under the arc lights you look up to the sound source and become aware of the pyramid glowing softly above, and then of the people beyond who stand in soft chiaroscuro. Acclimatised, you turn and look back towards the brightly lit space, to see people who now seem to linger unaccountably in that brightness, volumetrically surreal in the arc light that burns away shadow to make everything

geometrically expressive – like a small-scale Léger – or that burns away detail to make the essential more evident, as does the artificial lighting in film.

You feel free here, behind the veil of light, to stare at the newcomers, knowing you cannot be seen. Then, as you watch, these people move, as you did, towards the sound, pausing at the threshold, looking up as you did, to the sound. At this moment they are in complete silhouette, no detail is apparent, accentuating a caricature line as they stand, their chins upstretched, assembled in pairs and solitaires of marionette-like outlines. They are, for the moment, more revealed than ever they are when all the detail is available to us. Then they walk on and dim into chiaroscuro, and interact with the larger group, becoming part of a crowd of friends, colleagues and critics.

These deceptively simple layers of light, sound, performance and urban history weave one of the most captivating installations of the year. There is something about the specificity of the intention that makes it more telling than the more technically interesting but otherwise generic installations that offer little else. Is it too far-fetched to see in this a play of architectural reality, a reality that reaches to the metropolitan or general through a provincial, or local, actuality? ⊿

Professor Leon van Schaik is innovation professor of architecture at the Royal Melbourne Institute of Technology (RMIT). He works internationally with practitioners who have established mastery in their field, engaging them in critical review of the nature of their mastery, its enabling structures, its knowledge bases and the implications of the nexus between these for emerging forms of research-led practice. His latest book is *The Practice of Practice: Research in the Medium of Design* (RMIT Press, Melbourne, 2003).

Icebergs

Sheridan Rogers explains how Lazzarini Pickering and Tanner Architects have collaborated with restaurateur Maurice Terzini to create Icebergs, a restaurant located on Bondi Beach, Sydney's favourite stretch of waterfront.

Situated high on the sandstone cliffs at the southern end of Bondi Beach is Sydney's most stunning new venue, the Iceberg Dining Room and Bar. Designed by Rome-based Lazzarini Pickering Architetti in association with Sydney-based Tanner Architects, the interior captures the very essence of Bondi Beach. Whether sitting on one of the woven loom chairs in the restaurant or standing at the colour-backed glass bar, the experience of being surrounded by sea and sand is intense, captured by the clever use of interior mirrors that exploit a sense of spaciousness, and fabrics that echo the colour of the sea, sky, the pool below and the sand (in all weathers).

According to Claudio Lazzarini and Carl Pickering, it was 'like writing a love letter to Sydney – it's about everything we love about Australia'. The original building was very run-down and under reconstruction when the architects were called in. They reorganised the interior for the restaurant and bar, which proved to be very difficult because it had

the proportions of a long, wide corridor, but was quite domestic in scale. 'I wanted it to have the casualness of a sophisticated beach house but with the formality of a restaurant, to create serene spaces that concentrated one's attention on the view, rather than a long thin space full of tables and chairs,' says restaurateur Maurice Terzini. 'As well, I didn't want people to feel unwelcome if they were dressed only in board shorts, T-shirt and thongs.'

This was something new for Terzini, who was best known for his signature dark, intimate spaces like Caffe e Cucina and the bohemian Melbourne Wine Room. 'All my other ventures have been very urban,' he says. 'They were high velocity whereas Icebergs is far more relaxed with a sophisticated homely feel. People can sit around and enjoy themselves for hours here. It's all about the beach, about being on the water.'

Over the past 10 to 15 years, Sydney has experienced a distinct trend towards emphasising light, space and view in restaurant interiors, evidence of the city beginning to discover its own spirit of place and relinquishing the tradition of dark, indoor dining inherited from the UK.

The use of colour is a departure for Lazzarini and Pickering, whose European projects (recent projects include two villas at Cap Ferrat on the French Riviera, the revamped look of Fendi's worldwide boutiques and one of the newest buildings in the historic centre of Prague) are much more subdued. Giving intimacy to the space was a challenge that was overcome by a number of elements – a curved screen of aluminium rods in the foyer, which sway in the breeze like wind chimes, lend a sensual feel, and the C-shaped seating structures, evocative of crystallised waves or elongated sun-loungers dilate the space and continue outside on to the terrace to decrease the separation between interior and exterior, helping to structure and reproportion the long balcony area.

As well, the dramatic natural landscape by day had to find its equivalent in an artificial landscape at night. Large chandeliers, with candle-like lamps that flicker at night, were custom-designed in circular and linear configurations as required for each particular space. In the bar area (to the left of the foyer), a place to see and be seen, subtly stepped platform floors help break up the space, as do the hanging wicker 'egg' chairs that swing from the ceiling. To the right of the foyer are two dining

areas, each with a different character. Dining Room 2 at the southern end is more intimate and quiet, while Dining Room 1 with its C-shaped seating structures is designed for larger, noisier tables. The acoustic ceiling had to ensure that the ambient character of each of these spaces would remain distinct and comfortable, even when full. The whole back wall of the restaurant, which houses the kitchen and service areas, is finished in dark hues to distinguish them from the restaurant spaces. The dark tones absorb light and minimise disruption of the restaurant atmosphere every time a door to or from a service area is opened, and also prevent reflections in the large glass doors at night, allowing a perfect view of the lit beach and pool across the sea to north Bondi.

The menu, too, is a reflection of the view – clean, fresh and light with dishes like oysters natural; chargrilled octopus with cucumber, lemon and extra virgin olive oil; warm salad of Moreton Bay Bugs, shaved artichoke, peas, potatoes and labna; and chargrilled wild barramundi with vongole, white wine and faro. Icebergs could very well become *the* classic Sydney restaurant. ⌂

Sheridan Rogers is a journalist, author, broadcaster and food stylist in Sydney. She has written four books, including *The Cook's Garden* (HarperCollins, 1992) and *Seasonal Entertaining* (HarperCollins, 1994). In recognition of her contributions to food writing, she has received several awards, among them the Award for Gastronomic Writing in 1992.

Subscribe Now

As an influential and prestigious architectural publication, *Architectural Design* has an almost unrivalled reputation worldwide. Published bimonthly, it successfully combines the currency and topicality of a newsstand journal with the editorial rigour and design qualities of a book. Consistently at the forefront of cultural thought and design since the 1960s, it has time and again proved provocative and inspirational – inspiring theoretical, creative and technological advances. Prominent in the 1980s for the part it played in Postmodernism and then in Deconstruction, Δ has recently taken a pioneering role in the technological revolution of the 1990s. With groundbreaking titles dealing with cyberspace and hypersurface architecture, it has pursued the conceptual and critical implications of high-end computer software and virtual realities. Δ

Δ Architectural Design

SUBSCRIPTION RATES 2004
Institutional Rate: UK £160
Personal Rate: UK £99
Discount Student* Rate: UK £70
OUTSIDE UK
Institutional Rate: US $240
Personal Rate: US $150
Student* Rate: US $105

*Proof of studentship will be required when placing an order. Prices reflect rates for a 2002 subscription and are subject to change without notice.

TO SUBSCRIBE
Phone your credit card order:
+44 (0)1243 843 828

Fax your credit card order to:
+44 (0)1243 770 432

Email your credit card order to:
cs-journals@wiley.co.uk

Post your credit card or cheque order to:
John Wiley & Sons Ltd.
Journals Administration Department
1 Oldlands Way
Bognor Regis
West Sussex PO22 9SA
UK

Please include your postal delivery address with your order.

All Δ volumes are available individually. To place an order please write to:
John Wiley & Sons Ltd
Customer Services
1 Oldlands Way
Bognor Regis
West Sussex PO22 9SA

Please quote the ISBN number of the issue(s) you are ordering.

Δ is available to purchase on both a subscription basis and as individual volumes

○ I wish to subscribe to Δ *Architectural Design* at the **Institutional rate of £160.**

○ I wish to subscribe to Δ *Architectural Design* at the **Personal rate of £99.**

○ I wish to subscribe to Δ *Architectural Design* at the **Student rate of £70.**

○ Payment enclosed by Cheque/Money order/Drafts.

Value/Currency £/US$ _____

○ Please charge £/US$ _____
to my credit card.
Account number:

☐☐☐☐☐☐☐☐☐☐☐☐☐☐☐

Expiry date:

☐☐☐☐☐

Card: Visa/Amex/Mastercard/Eurocard *(delete as applicable)*

Cardholder's signature _____

Cardholder's name _____

Address _____

_____

_____ Post/Zip Code _____

Recipient's name _____

Address _____

_____

_____ Post/Zip Code _____

I would like to buy the following issues at £22.50 each:

○ Δ 166 *Club Culture*, Eleanor Curtis
○ Δ 165 *Urban Flashes Asia*, Nicholas Boyarsky + Peter Lang
○ Δ 164 *Home Front: New Developments in Housing*, Lucy Bullivant
○ Δ 163 *Art + Architecture*, Ivan Margolius
○ Δ 162 *Surface Consciousness*, Mark Taylor
○ Δ 161 *Off the Radar*, Brian Carter + Annette LeCuyer
○ Δ 160 *Food + Architecture*, Karen A Franck
○ Δ 159 *Versioning in Architecture*, SHoP
○ Δ 158 *Furniture + Architecture*, Edwin Heathcote
○ Δ 157 *Reflexive Architecture*, Neil Spiller
○ Δ 156 *Poetics in Architecture*, Leon van Schaik
○ Δ 155 *Contemporary Techniques in Architecture*, Ali Rahim
○ Δ 154 *Fame and Architecture*, J. Chance and T. Schmiedeknecht
○ Δ 153 *Looking Back in Envy*, Jan Kaplicky
○ Δ 152 *Green Architecture*, Brian Edwards
○ Δ 151 *New Babylonians*, Iain Borden + Sandy McCreery
○ Δ 150 *Architecture + Animation*, Bob Fear
○ Δ 149 *Young Blood*, Neil Spiller
○ Δ 148 *Fashion and Architecture*, Martin Pawley
○ Δ 147 *The Tragic in Architecture*, Richard Patterson
○ Δ 146 *The Transformable House*, Jonathan Bell and Sally Godwin
○ Δ 145 *Contemporary Processes in Architecture*, Ali Rahim
○ Δ 144 *Space Architecture*, Dr Rachel Armstrong
○ Δ 143 *Architecture and Film II*, Bob Fear
○ Δ 142 *Millennium Architecture*, Maggie Toy and Charles Jencks
○ Δ 141 *Hypersurface Architecture II*, Stephen Perrella
○ Δ 140 *Architecture of the Borderlands*, Teddy Cruz